Betty Jane Wylie

Enough

Lifestyle and Financial Planning for Simpler Living

Northstone

Editors: Michael Schwartzentruber, Sally Bryer Mennell
Cover and interior design: Margaret Kyle
Consulting art director: Robert MacDonald

A small portion of Chapter 1 of this book has been previously published in
"Facts & Arguments," in the *Globe and Mail*, November 1995.

We acknowledge the financial support of the Government of Canada through
the Book Publishing Industry Development Program for our publishing activities.

Northstone Publishing Inc. is an employee-owned company, committed to
caring for the environment and all creation. Northstone recycles, reuses and composts,
and encourages readers to do the same. Resources are printed on recycled paper and more
environmentally friendly groundwood papers (newsprint), whenever possible.
The trees used are replaced through donations to the Scoutrees for Canada Program.
Ten percent of all profit is donated to charitable organizations.

Canadian Cataloguing in Publication Data
Wylie, Betty Jane, 1931-
Enough

Includes bibliographical references and index.
ISBN 1-896836-18-6
1. Simplicity. II. Finance, Personal. I. Title
HG179.W948 1998   646.7   C98-910168-1

Published by Northstone Publishing Inc.
Kelowna, BC

Printing 10 9 8 7 6 5 4 3 2 1

Printed in Canada by Transcontinental Printing, Inc.
Peterborough, Ontario

To Ben Roberts, who makes it possible.

CONTENTS

Acknowledgments

Nothing is simple, especially trying to remember all the people who have helped me with this book. First of all, Christopher Cottier, for his enthusiasm and support; then all the people I met on the Net for their input, information and swift response. Numerous people gave me permission to quote, either in whole or in part, their material, including Tracy Axelsson (her car budget template), Tim Cestnick (from a special to the *Globe and Mail*, August 30, 1997), Donella H. Meadows and David Copeland (*If the World Were a Village*), Tony Presutto (the *Baking Soda* book), and the Funeral and Memorial Societies of America (FAMSA). My thanks also to Bob Darling of Investors' Group for his capsule history of mutual funds. Personal (by E-mail and phone) contacts include Peter Flemington, Joy Kogawa, Michael Linton, Michael Shapcott, and my bookseller Charlotte Stein (always!), and all the friends, relatives and acquaintances, plus my cohorts on the TWUC (The Writers' Union of Canada) listserv whose brains I pick daily. It truly is a worldwide web!

Preface

You who are in the midst of life and living it, or maybe feeling dragged along by it, you wonder what I can tell you that will be of any use. I have lived two-thirds of my life and have, if not solved, at least stumbled through most of the problems you are in the midst of. (Just bear in mind that I intend to go on for another third.) If you were forced to analyze all the pressures that are bugging you, you think they could probably be reduced to two things, both of which I must have plenty of by now. You also have a sneaking suspicion that they may be interchangeable as you try to play one off against the other. I'm talking, of course, about time and money.

You will say that I have reached the stage where I have more time and need less money, with my children grown, house paid for, and a wealth of memories to sustain me. Do remember that I still have to provide for the remaining third of my life: make a living as long as I can, come up with enough energy, my own or the purchased services of others, to take care of myself, and still put enough away to buy firewood for when I am really old and grey and nodding by the fire. I must use my time well, not merely cramming for my exams, as the saying goes, but choosing wisely how to spend it. Have you noticed that people use the verb *to spend* with time as well as money, knowing instinctively that the sage expenditure of both ultimately defines life? If only life were simple, it might be easier to define. Ay, there's the rub. If it were, I wouldn't be writing this book, nor you reading it.

What I have to say involves using time well and making the most of it. I will also talk about money, how to use it well and do with less of it. I seem to have a simple equation here: Time makes money; money buys time. Doing with less of one and more with the other makes the world go round, or vice versa, slower or faster as people get busier and busier, playing one thing off against the other, running short of both, feeling cheated of both. I think I will have to consider the psychology of money and evaluate the expenditure of time. It looks like a full plate. I hope to lick it clean as I try to control its contents, assess its durability, appraise its pleasures and savor its satisfactions. Not simple. However, my goal is simplicity. This is enough, for now.

PART I

Introduction

How much is enough?

1

My Story

You must live within yourself
and depend on yourself,
always tucked up and ready to go.
– Henry David Thoreau

A dozen years ago I was living in an expensive three-bedroom, two-bathroom, co-op apartment in Toronto, complete with 24-hour doorman, a whirlpool, and indoor and outdoor swimming pools. Although I had no mortgage payments nagging at me, maintenance fees were escalating, rising twice a year to pay for constant improvements and repairs and the high cost of security. I was running hard just to stay in place. To all appearances I was very successful. In the previous year I had published four books and had four book tours, three in Canada and one in the United States, from which I returned hoarse, tired and broke. Publishers pay travel expenses but they don't compensate for lost time, the myth being that the author will make it up in subsequent royalties as a result of the book being so well promoted. While the promotion goes on there isn't enough time or energy to generate new work for immediate income. I went six months without anything coming in, cashing in CSBs (Canada Savings Bonds) to live on. By the end of the year I was angry.

"If I'm so smart," I asked myself, "why aren't I rich?" That's when I decided to move.

My accountant encouraged me. (Well, he's not *my* accountant, but he calms my nerves every spring when I have to figure out my income tax.) He had noticed that over the years I did the bulk of my writing on retreat, in isolated places where I could work without distraction or temptation. Even though the places came free or with minimum charges for accommodation, I still had to get to them. My advisor suggested that I could buy my own retreat and stop spending so much money and time in the air, and I agreed. It took a while to find my hideaway and clear a path to it.

A dozen years before that, when I left our home in Stratford after my husband died, I staged the biggest garage sale in the world, which paid for the move to Toronto. My four children were still with me then, the oldest (girls) just off to university but home for holidays, so I needed that big apartment which was to become so excessive. When I moved that first time, I got rid of my future. Twelve years later I had to get rid of my past, which takes longer.

It takes time to scale down and divest oneself of possessions it took a lifetime to accumulate – time, plus a lot of decisions, memories and pain. By then, of course, my children were older with homes of their own so they got first crack at the stuff. My youngest, Matthew, was just moving into an apartment and could use the hide-a-bed sofa, end and coffee tables, his bedroom furniture, sheets, towels, dishes, pictures and so on. John was in his first house and able to take a few chairs, my bedroom furniture, books and some of my more esoteric cooking utensils. Kate, in Boston, received the Minton china and the silver hollowware (she had her grandmother's flatware), family mementoes (she's the archivist), and a few cookbooks. Liz accepted the Rosenthal china and the teak dining room suite. After that I had to work at it. This time I didn't have a garage to use as an unloading center. Nevertheless, I began an even more serious easing of the burdens.

It wasn't merely simplicity or extra cash I was looking for. I needed to pare down in order to squeeze into a summer cottage, never designed to hold a year-round wardrobe, luggage, or Christmas ornaments, let alone the linens, china, silver and crystal I owned for serious entertaining. I used to have a rule when the kids were little: no sterling silver in the sandbox. I extended the rule to summer cottages. So I sold all my silver and a complete set of crystal to a dealer – for very little, but enough to buy a new vacuum cleaner and a new water intake pump. The classifieds earned me more on special pieces: sterling silver oyster forks, parfait spoons, a Stilton cheese scoop, the remains of my grandmother's Belleek china and other precious bibelots. I sent dinner china and silver plate as well as all my mother's and grandmothers' cherished teacups, and my antique hanging lamps to an auctioneer (and was cheated because he ignored my reserve bids), and gave paintings and ornaments to my church bazaar. I sold curtains and accessories to the people who bought my apartment. I took bags of clothes and cartons of make-up and costume jewelry to a women's hostel, and carloads of miscellaneous treasures to charity flea markets. I sold the Harvard Classics and other good books to used book stores but John got my grandmother's sets of Thackeray, Dickens, Dumas, London and Twain; I kept her Shakespeare. I sold 30 years of *Gourmet* magazines, with the indices, to a magazine and paperback store, along with a complete collection of *Ms*, except for the launch issue (piggyback in *New York* magazine), which I still have.

I must admit books were, have been, still are, my biggest problem. Every available wall space is covered with bookcases and I have kept devising other spaces. Within a week of my moving in, the middle of the floor sagged and doors were sticking so Ben Roberts put a jack under a beam and braced it on a rock under the cottage which had no basement. Remember that name; every would-be simplifier has to have a Ben Roberts, someone who makes possible the new life you're trying to lead and who knows about plumbing.

The books continue to flow into my house and I can't seem to stop them, although as I have been working on this book I have finally realized that I am a serious bookaholic requiring a Twelve-Step ladder to get at all my treasures. At least my son bolted all the bookcases to the wall so none will tumble on me as I climb. I feel absolved by Mahatma Gandhi who comforted another biblio-addict who confessed he couldn't part with his books.

"Then don't give them up," Gandhi said. "As long as you derive inner help and comfort from anything, you should keep it. If you were to give it up in a mood of self-sacrifice or out of a stern sense of duty, you would continue to want it back, and that unsatisfied want would make trouble for you. Only give up a thing when you want some other condition so much that the thing no longer has any attraction for you, or when it seems to interfere with that which is more greatly desired."[1]

Oddly, I find that, as far as I'm concerned, this advice applies only to books. With an admittedly genuine but relatively painless wrench I gave away precious possessions, not only to my children but to friends, and feel completely at peace with the parting. I know exactly where the treasures are and it comforts me that someone else is enjoying them. At the same time, if people (usually my kids) feel the need to get rid of something I've given them, that's okay too. When I give something away, it's gone.

Actually, it's a nice feeling, one I recognized when I read about Diogenes and his bowl. You remember the story of the Greek philosopher who went looking for an honest man (or woman?), possessing nothing but his begging bowl for food to keep him alive. One day he stumbled and fell and broke his bowl.

"At last!" he said. "I'm free!"

As I say, it's a nice feeling.

I digress. I am still telling you how I pared down. After the bedroom furniture moved out, I turned ruthless. I had saved mementoes and souvenirs all my life, in fact, my entire life was documented in scrapbooks up to 1967 and in boxes after that, all of which took up most of the space in the apartment locker. I had always intended to commit the contents of the boxes to scrapbooks but now I dragged everything up to the floor of my empty bedroom and proceeded to toss my life into green garbage bags, reducing the detritus of a lifetime to judiciously chosen tokens (still occupying several boxes). I sat on the carpet with a bottle of wine and relived my past, drowning in maudlin reminiscence. It took several nights but I didn't become a wino.

As I filled a shoe box with some odds and ends of my grandmother's – old dance cards and programs, letters from her father on interesting letterheads from his travels, an old state fair paperweight, and so on, for all of which I received $150 from a used book and antique dealer – I remember wondering if I was denying a future granddaughter of mine some valuable source of income from my mementoes. There'll be other things.

As I went through this vast purge I was both exhilarated and frightened. I developed a terrible pain in my right hip and leg which took over a year and exercise plus a dedicated chiropractor to get rid of and which others might scoff at and say was only sciatica but which I became convinced was a very bad pun on my body's part. I was *dragging my foot*, I was *keeping one leg in the other room of my life*, afraid of the next step. It stopped hurting when I finally completed the move.

It took about a year and a half to do it, from the time I sold the co-op. I rented a one-bedroom apartment, used the bedroom as an office, and bought a futon on a frame to be my sofa bed in the living room. I had bruises the first month after I moved from bumping into walls and furniture in my cramped quarters. Meanwhile I was searching for my sanctuary.

First I visited friends who lived in the general area I had in mind, spending a night with each of them to give time for me to ask and them to answer my questions. The first ones were a couple who had settled in the woods and later in a small town where they were rearing their children. I knew I wanted a lakeshore property with lots of trees and rocks but no grass, enough wall space for books, and a fireplace. My friends cautioned me to look for a municipally plowed and sanded road, mail service, garbage pickup, a hot line on the water intake, and a short, flat driveway into my place so I wouldn't get stuck in the winter. Even sylvan retreats must have their practical aspects.

My other consultant had been widowed fewer years than I but had been able to move about more freely because she owned two homes, one in Florida and one on an Ontario lake. It happened that she and her husband had sold their city home shortly before his death so she had no permanent quarters in Toronto and was occupying various temporary digs to which she commuted freely. Mainly I wanted to know what it was like to spend so much time on the 400 (the lethal highway from lake country into the city) but ended up suggesting that we share rented accommodation in Toronto for the brief periods either of us planned to spend there – not together, but separately, in a bachelor apartment that served us well for ten years.

I mention this detail because that little studio with a galley kitchen gave me an escape hatch and a relatively inexpensive means of maintaining contacts in the city with family, friends and business, which I was still conducting. Of course, the cost of it earned me tax credits because I came in only for business; anything personal was a bonus after the original commitment. I was not retiring, remember, I was merely withdrawing, not the same thing. If you are considering such a major move as mine it might be wise not to close all your exits behind you. At the same time, you don't want to spend too much money on a backup living plan.

I'm getting ahead of myself. I was still looking for my new home. I found a real estate agent in the area and drove up weekends for her to take me around to various lakes while I looked for and she clarified my priorities. Then I took my older son to crawl and climb around houses and properties to check things out. But when I found my place, practical considerations (almost) flew out the window. I fell in love.

I walked into this room I am writing in now and heard music. Three walls of glass overlooking trees and water like those magic casements of Keats' *Ode to a Nightingale* – "opening on the foam/Of perilous seas, in faery lands forlorn" – transcended any practical considerations of heating (electric and expensive) or insulation (too thin). Luckily, this sun room I call a studio had been added on to a standard three-bedroom cottage and was the best-built room in the house, and the warmest, with a separate thermostat. My son pronounced the building secure and yes, it had the right kind of entrance drive and a fireplace. A few weeks later, after all the paperwork was done and I had the keys in my hand, I walked back into this room and heard the music again. I was home. I am home.

Of course, this kind of move would be impossible without the wire, the slim electric line that gives me knowledge and heat. Finally I understood what Marshall McLuhan meant when he said that "the electric light is pure information." By electric light I see and read and write well before and beyond daylight hours. I need more than light to write: I don't use a quill pen, and there aren't enough Bics in the world. The first thing I had to buy for my computer was a battery. Forget the power surge protector; this is brown- and blackout *insurance*. When the light line gets zapped, my expensive, large battery reassuringly gives me half an hour to save, back up, and exit.

I heard the expression *electronic cottager* before I became one, but the term doesn't half define the state. Unless I have to go into the village (10 kilometers away) to pick up milk or mail letters I don't get a newspaper, so I must rely on radio and television for my daily news and weather reports and entertainment (no horror shows; I have no intention of paralyzing myself with fear in my hideaway in the woods). Phone and fax enable me to communicate and conduct my business and now, just as I began the research for this book, another lifeline has become available. The Internet and E-mail have put my electronic fingers on the world's pulse. I am both wired and weird, and still dependent on power.

The round trip to the city is 400 kilometers. It costs me energy to go into the city: mine and that of a fossil fuel. Every time I agree to meet with a publisher or a producer, conduct or give an interview (depending on which side of the pencil I'm on), serve on a committee, sit on a board, or drive to the airport in order to fly to another city on business, I pollute the air and wear out the highway, my car and myself, so I am very careful to plan my trips and to cluster my work and appointments into packed visits. This two-hour drive has added another addictive item to my insatiable consumer's appetite: audio books. People ask me now, "Have you read suchandsuch?" and I answer, "No, but I've heard it."

I drink water too. Repeated tests have indicated that the water in my lake is no longer safe to drink unless it's boiled for ten minutes, a sad comment on the polluting effects of people. I tried a purifier but it wasn't satisfactory for too many reasons I won't go into. Now I have a water cooler in the kitchen and regular water delivery ($26 a month, depending on how much I drink) and must remember to eat well to make up for the essential trace minerals I'm missing. I get a fluoride treatment from my dentist once a year.

Light, heat, gas, water. No matter how simple one intends to be, one is still dependent for survival on sources outside oneself. Unless I want to be really drastic and head into the north woods to cope with a wood stove, outdoor facilities, and no running water at all, I must acknowledge my dependency on modern conveniences. I haven't mentioned food.

Last spring the only grocery store in my village burned to the ground, leaving the community as well as the poor owners devastated. As I write, building has begun on a new store which should be ready in a few months. In the meantime, with the co-operation of the community, the proprietors set up a grocery store in the arena so that local residents might be served. They moved very quickly, along with the hardware store owners, whose store and home above it were also destroyed in the fire, but it took about four weeks to get rolling. It happened that I had some major and pressing assignments that permitted little gadding about. I could not take the time to drive 45 kilometers to the nearest grocery store to stock up. (Tiny convenience stores in gas stations were closer but limited in selection and very expensive.) So I lived on what was in my admittedly well-stocked freezer, mostly cooked food, and ate very odd meals. When I ran out of birdseed (from the hardware store), I scattered bread crumbs for my outdoor pets. By the time the stores opened I was desperate for toilet paper. Another dependency!

I'm not complaining. I do love it – I'm still here, aren't I? But it's more expensive than I expected. Information and communication are the least of the high costs of the simple life. What I save on make-up and pantyhose I spend on electricity. The important, the paramount necessity here is to keep warm, to keep my personal lifelines from freezing. Warm in a winterized cottage is not like warm in a city high-rise. Simplicity like this involves some sacrifice and suffering, as well as considerable ingenuity.

Every January a cold war strikes and I huddle. My pipes and/or septic line freeze; my electric heaters stand like sentinels at the walls, valiantly trying to keep the frigid air outside at bay. The trick is to keep the body warm and not the whole house. Every morning I layer on a delicious assortment of clothes: cotton and Lycra® tights (English wool when I get serious), silk undershirts, big wool skirts, Ice-wool sweaters, socks, moccasins, heavy shawls, which I have stationed around the house for extra warmth. I look like a giant tea cosy. If I fell over I'd roll helplessly like Tweedledee and I have no Tweedledum to haul me to my feet.

My first winter I shut myself into a bedroom with an extra radiant heater aimed at my fingers so I could write on a clipboard. Before the next year shivered in I had the living room heaters replaced. Then a new laptop plus the radiant heater blew the circuits so I had the electric service to the house increased. I lit a fire every night – an aesthetic pleasure – and bought more wood, a ceiling fan to push the warm air down, had the chimney cleaned, and then had extra insulation blown into the walls. I bought kerosene lamps and lots of candles and extra fuel for my old fondue heater (it takes 27 minutes to boil a cup of water for tea) and special andirons and a lock-in grid so now I can cook over the fire when there's a power failure in the winter. Now when it happens, I'm so cosy that when the power comes back on, I remain basking in fire- and candlelight for the evening – but not every evening.

As each winter passes I gain deeper respect for our pioneering foremothers who worked so hard to keep their families healthy and warm during inexorable, unbelievable winters. I remember reading one North Dakota diarist, writing with a finger that had been frozen for two weeks, who described with pleasure and hope the promise of spring implicit in her budding fuchsia plant. I, too, have begun to cherish indoor plants.

The question arises with each new winter: why don't I go south? Of course, I've spent so much on my simple rural comforts that I can't afford to leave, but the truth is I don't want to. The secret of winter in the Muskokas is well kept by us year-rounders: it's breathtakingly beautiful. My favorite color combination is blue and white and that's what I get here: blue sky and white snow, and the white stays white. The green cathedral of trees that surround my cottage transmutes to a white temple, secret and silent. Simple. But it costs.

I've told you all this to try to indicate to you the first necessary steps if you're serious about scaling down your lifestyle. There are things you should be aware of before you go all misty-eyed about a "bee-loud glade." Voluntary simplicity, I discovered, can lead to involuntary complexity. Give it some thought.

PART II

Where Do We Go from Here?

The world is too much with us; late and soon,
Getting and spending, we lay waste our powers:
Little we see in Nature that is ours;
We have given our hearts away, a sordid boon!
– William Wordsworth

2

Running on Automatic

Trying to consume our way to prosperity,
we have been exhausting ourselves.
– Marilyn Ferguson

You see it all around you, the mad scramble. You and the people you know who are working, are working more and harder, putting in longer hours for less satisfaction and less money as family incomes decline. In 1993 Statistics Canada reported that an estimated 275,000 families (about 800,000 people) had disappeared from the ranks of the middle class since 1982.[1] Middle income is considered to be between $30,000 and $60,000 a year, or was; Canadian family income is now less than it was in 1980. As jobs disappear through forced early retirement and natural attrition, those left in the labor force work double time. More and more wives and mothers (over 50 percent of them) have added their efforts in work outside the home in an attempt to maintain previous levels of income or to meet the needs of a growing family. With new jobs scarce and money tight, a recession has gripped the economy until very recently. The economy is recovering and growing, we are told, but jobs are still scarce so that buying power has continued to shrink.

But is it only a lack of money that's bothering you? You may feel as if you're running frantically not for advancement but just to stay where you are, with less and less time for yourself and your family. Whatever happened to the Good Life? Define good life.

It's almost impossible to describe what's bothering you or what you'd like to do about it without bumping smack into a cliché. Being fully aware that your reach must exceed your grasp, you keep stretching for the brass ring even as you cry out for the world to stop so you can get off. You feel guilty because you don't take time to consider the lilies of the field and sniff the flowers as you rush by. Ruefully remembering the rich young man who couldn't take less for an answer, nevertheless you don't leave home without your credit cards, feeling as squeezed as that poor camel, with the eye of the needle upon you as you fall like a sparrow to the tired earth.[2] Is it supposed to be like this? Was it always? Maybe it was.

More than 20 years ago, before we had learned to name Beijing correctly, I went to see the Peking Man Exhibition at the Royal Ontario Museum where artifacts dating from thousands of years B.C. were on tour: a mummified king in his sarcophagus with his riches and necessities; jewelry, art and ornaments, including that horse sculpture seeming to run in mid-air (reproduced for sale in the Museum gift shop); shards of clay dug out of burial mounds and pieced together along with miraculously whole pots with their decoration still visible after all these centuries. I remember looking at them, the oldest manmade things I had ever seen, while I pondered the human drive for embellishment and accumulation. It seems that as soon as people have a pot to pee in, they decorate it and want two. Nothing is simple.

Trying to keep up with Peking Man, we still do that. It's a human drive. The late Doris Janzen Longacre, author of *Living More with Less*, says that even today "the plainest cooking area behind a hut in Somalia boasts an intricately carved stool or colorful basket." We acquire, we bedeck, and we acquire more, never noticing or perhaps not caring that we are caught up in a mad scramble for possessions until we are not only possessed but obsessed. That's part of it, human materialism and acquisitiveness, part of what drives and owns us. It's gum-on-the-bedpost thinking.

Maybe you didn't do this when you were a kid, but I used to collect gum. In my mouth. I would add to the wad each day and every night I stuck it on the bedpost where it dried out just enough to make it a challenging chew the next morning. This was in the summer; in the winter I went to a convent school where no young lady could be caught dead with gum in her mouth. One day I was walking back from the well with a bucket of water (I was with my family at a summer cottage with no plumbing), chewing and singing and pulling my gum with my free hand to see how far it would stretch, when a fish fly landed on the gum-line. Not wanting to drop the water, but with my only free hand holding the end of the gum, I tried to disentangle the fish fly and retain my gum. By the time I returned to the cottage with half a pail of water and sodden shoes, I had only a tiny chaw of gum left. I think that was my first lesson in the hazards of excessive accumulation.

Essentially what people are doing who amass more stuff than they need is accumulating gum. When the really big gum-wadders have bitten off more than they can chew, that is, run out of private space to store it, they give it to galleries and museums (for a tax break) and share their enthusiasm with others. Not all exhibition places are thus privately endowed, of course. We have public ones, too, run with public funding. Failing one's own art and artifacts, we all love to look at others'. Museums are the bedposts of civilization, gathering places where we can admire collections of gum, or whatever. It's a benign fetish. I'd much rather we accumulate gum than guns. The point I'm making here is that human beings have always tended to surround themselves with more and fancier stuff than they need if they possibly can, at whatever price they can afford. So when we groan and point fingers at current conspicuous consumption, it's not a new excess people have suddenly developed.

As you might expect, there have always been cautious heads with tsk-ing tongues, reminding their extravagant fellow creatures that less is more, treasures are best laid up in the hearts of others or in heaven, whichever comes first, and simpler ways lead to peace of mind and heart's ease. Soul's ease too. Nothing much has changed, it seems. We keep on needing to be reminded. Maybe this time it would be a good idea to pay attention to the tongue-cluckers. The world is not only too much with us, it's full. Time is running out, not only time but also earth, air, water, fossil fuels, ozone, food and patience. When we talk voluntary simplicity now, it's time to listen before it becomes involuntary and we become obsolete.

Simplicity is not a new idea. Plato had a firm grasp of it when he reported Socrates' words.

> *I do nothing but go about persuading you all, old and young alike,*
> *not to take thought for your persons or your properties, but first and chiefly to*
> *care about the greatest improvement of the soul. I tell you that virtue*
> *does not come from money, but that from virtue comes money*
> *and every other good of man, public as well as private.*
> – Plato's Apology

It may seem you've read something like this elsewhere:

> *Lay not up for yourselves treasures upon earth, where moth and rust doth*
> *corrupt, and where thieves break through and steal: But lay up for yourselves*
> *treasures in heaven. For where your treasure is, there will your heart be also.*
> – Matthew 6:19–21

Many of the great, simple philosophers and thinkers of history have said much the same thing. The question is, when are we going to pay attention?

As long as there have been excesses there have been ascetics, selfless nonconformists like Confucius, Socrates, Jesus, St. Francis, Sir Thomas More, Joan of Arc, Julian of Norwich, Leo Tolstoy (but he wasn't good to his wife), Mark Twain, Henry David Thoreau, Albert Schweitzer, Etty Hillesum, Mahatma Gandhi, E. F. Schumacher,[3] Mother Teresa and Vicki Robin, people who lived what most of us only profess to believe.

There have always been countermovements, swings toward simple living and the thoughtful use of resources. A student of history can come up with the names of any number of closed communities, mini-societies devoted to simple living and high thinking, often grounded in a nonconformist religion. North America was first settled by people who were seeking freedom of expression in their religion and whose lifestyles usually corresponded to their austere commandments. The names are familiar: Quaker, Puritan, Amish, Old Order Mennonite, Mormon, Hutterite, Doukhobor, not to mention spin-off groups like the Oneida or Shaker communities and the stranger cults of recent times. In one way or another they all deplore and renounce the temptations and potential damage of the material world while attempting to substitute some kind of alternative lifestyle and discipline (which can lead to a different kind of excess). Not to pursue any of the religious tenets, per se, I just want to follow the line of simple thinking to this not-so-new impasse we have reached, an idea whose time has come and come and come again.

As far as we are concerned right now with the newest ripple of this centuries-old wave, the term *voluntary simplicity* has been credited to Richard Gregg, an American Quaker, who in 1936 used it to describe a lifestyle which concentrated on things that really matter – an ambiguous definition. "The degree of simplification," Gregg said, "is a matter for each individual to settle for himself." This, of course, allows for tremendous leeway because what matters lies in the preference of the consumer. Gregg was wise enough to recognize the difficulties involved for an ordinary mortal struggling to be simple. Hard enough to be plain! "Simplicity," he said, "seems to be a foible of saints and occasional geniuses, but not something for the rest of us." Define simplicity. We're going to try.

Elaine St. James, author of three books, so far, on simple living, pared down her wardrobe but kept on driving her beloved old Beemer. I know someone who loves to travel and eat well but who doesn't care where he sleeps, choosing the cheapest digs he can find while he dines at four-star restaurants. A recent item in a newspaper clarified Clint Eastwood's attitude to conspicuous consumption: "I don't have a lot of needs. I drive cars that are older. If I find something I like, I usually keep it. I have a helicopter I like very much."

There you are.

Voluntary simplicity, it seems, is not a lifestyle but a mindset. Marilyn Ferguson, bestselling author of *The Aquarian Conspiracy* (1980 – another cult book), concurs with this idea. "Voluntary simplicity," she writes, "is an attitude, not a budget: thoughtful consumption, resistance to artificially created 'needs,' sensitivity to the limits of natural resources, a more human scale for living and working." If you find yourself nodding in agreement, you're riding the crest of a new wave, or maybe it's the new crest of an old wave.

There's no doubt we're surfing now, with the Internet to help us. The information highway is crammed with Web sites and home pages filled to their earnest epiglottises with lectures, explanations, sermons, tips, hints, sources and resources, contacts and kits all designed to help you find your way to nirvana, or if not nirvana, plain living and high thinking at the lowest prices available. Unfortunately, advocates fall short when they try to stuff spiritual salvation, ecological altruism, hairshirt hedonism and tightwad tactics all into one glorious metaphysical ball for hurling at the politicians and corporations who are spoiling our sandbox, Earth. Each guru, economist or penny pincher has a fraction of the action and believes that it is the only way to go. Actually, it's a fascinating amalgam and one is beguiled into wishing it could all come together, or at least stop moving long enough to take a good look – hence this book.

There are two branches to this stream, or two crests to the wave, to stay with the metaphor. On the one hand, there is the earnest, philosophical, ecologically pure idealist who hopes to save the planet, raise perfect children and savor the simple life, without it costing an arm and a leg, literally. On the other hand, there is an earnest, hardheaded, business-minded pragmatist who hopes to save the bacon, raise a perfect child and savor the simple life, without it costing an arm and a leg, financially. What I hope to do is present a rounded picture; not only a rose-spectacled view of simplicity but also a clear-eyed assessment of how to make it work for thoughtful North Americans. No one can just drop off the edge of a world that is not only not flat but terribly round and convoluted. The best any of us can hope for is to make our little space as smooth as possible.

When American economist Duane Elgin published a book entitled *Voluntary Simplicity* in 1981, he became the new guru for the next two decades, the one most often cited as the father of it all, this time round. Basically, Elgin advocates a simpler lifestyle: reducing consumption in order to preserve the world's resources and reducing stress in order to increase personal fulfillment. Stop running so hard and so long for pay and spend more time with children, family, friends and the community. But can you afford it? Elgin's book has inspired a whole network (The Simple Living Network) of followers, a regularly published *Journal of Voluntary Simplicity* (see Appendix 1), and any number of spin-offs.

The most successful simple living book of this decade has been *Your Money or Your Life: Transforming Your Relationship with Money and Achieving Financial Independence* (600,000 copies sold since its publication in 1992, and updated), by Vicki Robin and the late Joe Dominguez (d. January 1997). The two estimated their cost of living at $500 a month for 20 years, but made so embarrassingly much money with their book that they set up a nonprofit foundation – the New Road Map Foundation – dedicated to promoting a simple lifestyle for everyone. Robin lives now on about $7,000 a year. She has enough, she says, living in shared housing and driving her 1984 Toyota Tercel for which she changes the oil and spark plugs herself. Now that's awesome! So is having enough.

YMOYL, as it is known, offers a nine-step program to financial independence, creating a system to take care of your basic needs before you go out to save the planet. It's a business book with soul, required reading for those intent on making dollars and sense of their spiritual drive toward simplicity without jeopardizing the future of the next generation. What we all need to do is tether the high-flying, none-too-practical spirits while giving wings to the mundane plodders.

The entire movement now is riddled with memes.[4] Slick phrases and undigested ideas are bandied about as easily as a cap is turned bill-backward to look hip. You'll be told to "de-junk" your life, get rid of the clutter, toss the *tchotchkes*. *Tightwad Gazette* magazine, now defunct, led to the publication of books with the same title, volumes I, II and III, and made a million dollars for its creator, Amy Dacyczyn (pronounced "decision"). You will also find a *Cheapskate Monthly*, *The Dollar Stretcher* weekly, a *Simple Living* journal, *Country Connections* magazine, and the *GreenMoney Journal*, each with its own spin, lots of homely housekeeping tips to save time and money, all aimed at conscious, conscientious living habits. You could spend a fortune on the magazines alone, almost 30 of them at my last count, devoted to saving money! They all warn you about conspicuous consumption; the flip side, inconspicuous consumption, is not without its own pitfalls.

A breathtakingly beautiful issue of *Home Design*, in a summer 1997 *New York Sunday Times*, was dedicated to inconspicuous consumption. Catching fire from the voluntary simplicity movement, the idea once again is that "less is more," the maxim attributed to the German-born, American architect Mies van der Rohe, but originating with poet Robert Browning (from his 1855 poem, "Andrea del Sarto").

It's very cool right now not to be ostentatious in the display of what money can buy. Everyone who's anyone is throwing up their collective hands in dismay and horror at the profligate spending of the 1980s. I don't know how this righteous repugnance sits with the recent flamboyant purchases of the late Princess Diana's cast-off clothes; I guess expenses like that are justified as recycling – on a grand scale. Anyway, why am I not surprised that "unassuming elegance" costs? Other meaningful phrases include: conscious consumerism, living more with less, upshifting (meaning the same as downshifting, basically a pattern shifting to a different, simpler lifestyle with the emphasis on spiritual development), and living with balance, also known as living gently, or living lightly on Earth. Ecology is never far behind.

The emphasis of the movement seems to be on materialistic solutions, suggestions for solving the financial problems of downsizing (another variation of the catch term), enlightened investing, low-fat cooking, cheap cleaning and shopping tips that everyone can understand. From there it's an easy step to coupons, thence to barter, to swapping, to trading, and eventually to community currency, a very large idea that is rapidly becoming high finance and political in its nature.

At the same time, the spiritual aspect is running alongside, supposedly justifying the hard line the virtual currency people are taking, if anyone cared to seek justification. Enough for the moment to be simpler than thou, taking the high thinking road to heaven, passing, no doubt, through an ozone layer we're going to have to do something about sooner than later. We're going with the flow.

Mihaly Csikszentmihalyi is a psychologist and the bestselling author of *Flow: The Psychology of Optimal Experience* (1990). In his sequel, *The Evolving Self: A Psychology for the Third Millennium* (1993), Csikszentmihalyi, searching for the faith that will enable us to go on into the future, recommends not a simplicity, but a complexity of consciousness. He identifies what he calls "flow experiences" as the source of our interests, abilities and goals. This may not sound simple but everyone has a click of recognition when flow is described (almost literally, as in "go with the flow"!), a kind of mental overdrive when all systems are go.

Csikszentmihalyi offers four basic axioms as a guide to our thinking for the future, quite simple, really, based on what you are and already know. They are the most effective clarification of what voluntary simplicity is all about, if it is to be taken seriously and not fade out like a fad at the end of this anxious, final decade of the second millennium. To recap what he says, simply: number one is a statement of your ecological responsibility; being part of the universe and the order of things, you hurt yourself if you mess it up. Number two recognizes your unique response to your particular space in time; not only are you special, you're it, right there in the middle of your self (like Jung's centerpoint). Everything you know is based on your own reactions and knowledge. Number three puts the onus directly on you for your actions; recognizing that everything you do comes from you, you are, therefore, totally responsible for what you do – if you let outside forces control what you do, you're missing the boat. Number four challenges you to keep on searching in this time frame – and beyond. Your trip, though never finished, will keep on defining you. Your evolving self must keep on transcending its own limits. Awareness, acceptance, responsibility, transcendence – they're not exactly new ideas, but it seems we have to keep on learning them.

This current drive to simplify our lives has everything to do with time – our time and the time we have left. When you're young, you have all the time in the world. As you grow older and more finite, so does time. Choices have consequences; second chances dwindle. You used to be a weather vane; now you are a pendulum, swinging back toward a future that draws closer all the time. You realize that it is not only possible, it is necessary to learn to say no.

3

Consumption

One man's consumption becomes his neighbor's wish.
– John Kenneth Galbraith

consume v.
1. eat or drink up.
2. destroy; burn up.
3. use up; spend: *A student consumes much of his time in studying.*
4. waste away; be destroyed.
5. waste (time, money, etc.).

consumption n.
1. the act of using or using up: *We took along some food for consumption on our trip. The science of economics deals with the production, distribution, and the consumption of wealth.*
2. the amount used up: *Our [power] hydro consumption was up again last month.*
3. a wasting disease of the lungs...[1]

I never take a word or an attitude for granted. I thought I knew what *consume* and *consumption* meant, but see what I learned – the significant use of the preposition *up* tacked on to indicate the thoroughness of the activity: eat *up*, drink *up*, burn *up*, use *up*. It's the opposite of our intended direction. We're supposed to be on our way *down*: *down* scaling, *down* shifting, *down* playing. Down, but not out.

There are several different approaches to consumption we should consider, and their effects. The first, of course, is conspicuous. One thinks of sleek limos, private planes, sparkling yachts, the Riviera, exquisite clothes, lavish parties with champagne bottles popping – all the clichés the movies have taught us to associate with blatant materialism. At the height of so-called conspicuous consumption there were strict rules about it that also became (crippling) clichés. You don't have to read Edith Wharton, you can see the movie based on her novel *The Age of Innocence*, and see the rules in action, beautifully illustrated. Sometimes when I look at that period in history – the end of the 19th century in North America – I think maybe I was born at the wrong time. With my luck, though, I'd have been a hired girl.

What about inconspicuous consumption? The big spenders hid their spending when it seemed wise to do so, concealing their comforts and extravagances during lean times or war time in order to avoid criticism and backlash. Inconspicuous spending didn't mean they were spending less, it just meant they weren't flaunting it. Maybe it was then that people began to consider asking the price of something, or telling it, as very low-class. Really high-class, old-school restaurants still give the woman the menu with no prices in the right-hand column. I don't like anything that gesture implies about women or money.

These days, in view of what we're doing to the planet, we all must think about over-consumption. Elsewhere I cite statistics that show what over-consumers North Americans are (see page 84), not only using up more of Earth's resources than the rest of the world, but using them up faster. We begin to understand the meaning of words like nonrenewable and irreplaceable. We are in real danger of using up everything to the point of running out.

Finally, because of the current fascination with this new trend, let's take a good hard look at conspicuous non-consumption. Is it only another trend? Is it merely chic simplicity?

Conspicuous Consumption

A private railroad car is not an acquired taste.
One takes to it immediately.
— Eleanor R. (Mrs. August) Belmont
(English actress & philanthropist)

The American economist Thorstein Veblen (1857-1929) was born in Wisconsin and grew up on a farm. He published *The Theory of the Leisure Class* in 1899, winning fame in literary as well as sociological circles. One wonders if he and Canadian-born economist John Kenneth Galbraith (himself now in his 90s) would have had an argument if they'd ever met. I think so. In his book *The Affluent Society* (1958), Galbraith blames Veblen and his cynical followers for scorning the notion that economic progress could do the masses any good. Veblen, of course, is the man who gave us the phrase "conspicuous consumption," which threw a glaring spotlight on the resented gap between the haves and the have-nots. Influenced by Veblen, pessimistic intellectuals resisted falling for reform or any improvements under the villain capitalism. Rich people – the conspicuous consumers – could never go through the eye of any needle. It took Roosevelt's New Deal reforms, distrusted at first, to dispel some of the fear and prejudice. Galbraith was always a champion of that kind of (Democratic) government spending, using more public money for public services and less of it for private consumption.

Galbraith seems to agree with Veblen about women, though. The earlier economist pointed out that as industrial society grew and the nuclear family (not his term) evolved, it fell to women to be not only the last servants, but also diligent consumers in order to make their menfolk look and feel powerful. Galbraith has commented on how well women have been taught to consume. Their shopping habits were essential to the economy. What happens when they (begin to) stop consuming? It's already having a profound effect.

Most societies in most centuries have had a leisure class, in some cases so conspicuous and profligate in their consumption as to be hated and killed (for example, the French aristocracy in the late 18th century; the Russian royal family at the beginning of the 20th century). Now the leisure class seems to have disappeared, at least, that idle, extravagant, feckless kind. Even Queen Elizabeth is selling her yacht. These days work for everyone is considered to be both respectable and necessary. This is not to say that all work is equal; we certainly know it is not recompensed equally. As we look at the stratospheric salaries of sports figures, rock and movie stars, and have only begun to notice the larger, longer-term rewards of CEOs, we are all too aware of pay inequities and of a denied, hidden but rock-bound caste system based on education, prestige and, of course, money. Money seems to be the way out of the trap. That's why lotteries were invented.

Barring a revolution and a total redistribution of income, found money still seems to be the only hope for the have-nots. People stopped believing in enchanted fishes and fairy godmothers when Magic Pools (lotteries) became available. What happens when Boots hits the jackpot? Do we expect him then to be careful? The television commercials advertising the various lotteries certainly don't. "Just imagine!" they sing, and show wild behavior and crazy spending – what you might even call conspicuous consumption. How can we expect people who have had to scrimp and save all their lives suddenly to become careful and wise when they have more money than they ever imagined? The very fact that lotteries (and casinos and pools and sweepstakes and all those dream-tickets to Shangri-La) exist means that people are still looking for the pot at the end of the rainbow. If or when they find it, they have every intention of spending it. This is probably why yet other surveys reveal that most lottery winners end up jobless, broke, divorced, alienated, beer-drinking louts on welfare. Downsizing still doesn't apply to them. They pull the rungs out of their own ladders. Who's to say we wouldn't act the same? When we talk about conspicuous consumption with wagging fingers and clucking tongues, just remember Peking Man. We have a long way to go.

Inconspicuous Consumption

Nothing that costs only a dollar is worth having.
~ Elizabeth Arden

It's easy to mock conspicuous consumption. We're going to have to work harder at understanding the inconspicuous kind. I'll tell you the nicest story I know about inconspicuous consumption, read long ago in one of the women's magazines when they still published fiction and I was not professional enough to notice the name of the writer.

A very shy, quiet young woman on the plain-to-mousy side worked at a mundane job, lived alone, fed her cat, dreamed a lot. Believing that clouds had silver linings, she did a strange thing. She bought a length of colorful silk sari cloth and carefully lined her workmanlike, beige-colored raincoat with it. No one knew or noticed, but she did, and that's what counted. She was a princess incognito. It was a love story, of course. A man noticed her eyes flashing at the sight of a street minstrel (or something – I'm making up this part), caught a glimpse of her sari lining and knew she was special. All right, corny, and the lady was too materialistic and romantic and not a good planner. She should have invested in mutual funds, which probably hadn't been invented when I read that story. I've carried the image ever since, though – to me the ultimate example of inconspicuous consumption. Maybe it says something about the attitude you should take with you into your new life. Deprivation is in the soul of the one who experiences it. So are joy and abundance. Look for the sari lining.

When I say deprivation, I'm not talking hunger and thirst or the kind of pain suffered in Third World countries and caused by a genuine lack of life's necessities and threats to people's lives. No matter how much anyone on this continent pares down, the depth of paring cannot reach as low as the bottom line anywhere else. Now I'll qualify that: I mean, anyone who is reading this book, toying with the idea of simplicity. This is, after all, a middle-class endeavor. We have a reasonable and civilized attitude, so we think, and a clear idea of the good life: uncluttered, unostentatious, simple. But comfortable. With a sari lining.

Over-Consumption

Some is good, more is better. Too much is just right.
– Great American Axiom[2]

You don't need me to tell you about over-consumption. All you have to do is pick up your newspaper each day and read about the trouble we're having finding landfill sites for all our trash. No one wants the trash but very few people so far are doing anything about lessening the load.

The Recycling Council of Ontario (RCO) has started to do something. Founded in 1978 with a mandate to promote reduction, reuse, recycling and composting in order to reduce waste, this nonprofit organization hands out annual Waste Minimization Awards and reports on the most successful and innovative ideas and programs that others might copy. Categories include: Outstanding Individual – Youth; Outstanding Individual – Adult; Outstanding School; Outstanding Educational Initiative; Outstanding Municipality (population less than 50,000); Outstanding Municipality (population more than 50,000); Outstanding Market Development; Outstanding Business; Outstanding Green Industry; Outstanding Institution; Outstanding Non-Profit Organization; Outstanding Recycling Program Operator; and a Committee Award, made at the discretion of the committee members recognizing the outstanding waste reduction of an individual or a community group or business. Most of the projects not only extend landfill site life by reducing the amount of waste, they also save and even make money through reuse and recycling.

The all-time big Chairman's Award recognizing the most significant overall achievement in the areas of waste reduction, reuse and recycling goes hands-down to the Brewers Retail Inc. of Ontario. Since 1927, the "Beer Store" has been recovering bottles for refilling, an estimated 60 billion beer bottles that might otherwise have gone to Ontario landfill sites. This is the best recovery program in the world, a deposit-refund incentive system resulting in a return rate of 98.8 percent on glass bottles and 97 percent on other types.

Another project of RCO, too new for the returns to be in, is the ReinCARnate Program. Recycle your car in Ontario, they say, and get a charitable tax receipt and a free tow. (How?)

Another new kind of incentive is developing through an old method – barter. Called a materials exchange service, first being used successfully in Tennessee where Dr. Richard Buggeln[3] has joined the state's Center for Industrial Services (CIS), to create and manage the Tennessee Materials Exchange (TME). "One company's waste can often be used in another company's manufacturing operation," says Buggeln. "The challenge is in letting them know what's out there and getting the interested parties together." He does this through the *Tennessee Materials Exchange Bulletin*.

The idea is to help entrepreneurs create new products from waste materials discarded by other industries. He's talking big stuff like scrap wood and cloth fibers, materials we can easily understand have a real potential for recycling. Less obvious is the arrangement between an instrument company in Rockwood, TN, which sends its waste glass to an asphalt company in Atlanta; the latter needs about exactly as much as the former company generates.

Perhaps you have seen in upscale gift stores something I noticed recently: keychain ornaments, clipboards and binder covers made from discarded, damaged computer boards, very hi-tech, very pricey. As we become more careful shoppers, this kind of thing may not appeal to us; in the meantime, give the designer A for effort for finding a new use for discarded material. Maybe you can get a keychain on sale. Or buy two, get one free.

You can probably quote a few more sales come-ons like that. Reduced 30% – why wait? All you can eat for $9.95. Shop till you drop. Buy now, pay later. These are the slogans we live with, urging us constantly to overspend and overconsume. Do we stop to think what we're doing to the planet?

The Worldwatch Institute offers an equation by which we can estimate the effect of a country on Earth's ecological system.

Factor in three variables:
- population size
- average consumption
- technologies used to provide the goods and services.

The United States (and by corollary Canada) is the most overpopulated country in the world. In terms of energy consumption, the 3 million Americans added to the population every year are equivalent to 90 million Indians.[4] If we are truly looking to establish sustainable living patterns, a simple life, then we must stop over-consumption. We can't grow anymore; we have to start maturing.

Conspicuous Non-Consumption

We've found the habit of asking
"Will this really simplify our lives?"
a powerful weapon in the ongoing battle
against the complications of modern life.
— Elaine St. James

The supreme irony is that the people who have led the way, the gurus and the role models, the ones who have most impressed us with their complete espousal of the simple life, have made a fortune doing it.

Elaine St. James won't say how much money she has made on her best-selling books[5] but she consciously avoids capitalizing on them; she turned down a few endorsements, including one from a pharmaceutical company pushing an antistress remedy. In that she was true to herself; Recommendation Number 66 in *Simplify Your Life: 100 Ways to Slow Down and Enjoy the Things That Really Matter* reads "Throw Out Everything but the Aspirin." She says if people changed their lifestyle, they wouldn't need relaxants.

Nevertheless, St. James is conspicuous in her non-consumption. She threw out all her clothes and reduced her wardrobe to two skirts, two blazers, two pairs of slacks, five T-shirts and six turtlenecks. But she drives a BMW

– used. It's like me and my books. As Gandhi says, enjoy! (Well, he didn't say that exactly, but that's what he meant.)

I have already reported that the tightwads, Amy and Jim Dacyczyn, made a ton more money by selling their saving ideas than they did by following them. Vicki Robin and the late Joe Dominguez grossed $3.5 million in the first three years their book *Your Money or Your Life* was in print, and plowed the money back into the New Road Map Foundation, continuing to live on about $500 (each) a month. Robin still honors her conspicuous non-consumption.

Lifestyles of the Abstemious and Famous? As St. James says, "It's an ongoing challenge to stay simple." Especially when it has become an industry. Or has voluntary simplicity, conspicuous as it now is, become a fad, a trend or a major societal movement? Perhaps it's a revolution.

PART III

Civilization in Transition

Quality of living is not the same as standard of living.
– Vicki Robin

4

Lifestyle and Livelihood

Values can get buried under a lifestyle.
– Vicki Robin

lifestyle n.
a way of life; the typical habits, pastimes, attitudes, etc.
of a person or group: *a casual lifestyle.*
Their downtown apartment suits their lifestyle.[1]

What the dictionary doesn't tell us are the stories behind a way of life. Habits are the result of a lifetime of often unconscious choices; pastimes are activities chosen according to preferences, tastes, training, custom. Attitudes have been carefully ingrained, almost part of one's character; it takes conscious choice to change them, and after that, real effort to change behavior. Most of us have been programmed, whether we realize it or not, genetically or economically or subliminally (see Media, p. 61). Just look at how many people end up (a) doing exactly what their parents did, or (b) not. Most of us are knee-jerks living out what we learned at our mother's knee, or some other low joint, as the saying goes. Did we ever have a choice? Do we now?

The dream of an ever-improving future seems naive to some of us today, particularly to the Generation Xers who will never see one long-term, stable job with a golden handshake and watch at the end of it. Yet their seniors, all the Boomers, the Big Generation born between 1946 and 1965, although moving from job to job and place to place in their search for the good life, still act as if they do believe. (For good life read: lifestyle.) They think they have made a conscious choice or choices. Every dream is still theoretically possible as long as they observe the rules. If they offer a significant payment – of time, effort, money – then the goal can be achieved. Anyone's dream can come true when you wish upon a star, and work hard.

In the meantime, the average work week, once shorter thanks to the turn-of-the century strikes that made the workplace more lucrative and less hazardous, has grown longer. Flexible time has turned into marathon schedules: 12 hours on for three days, and four days off to recover. The less fortunate are offered early retirement, a euphemism for being laid off; part-time jobs are offered (take it or leave it), catering especially to wives' and mothers' other time demands, with no benefits. The choice has been to work harder and longer for less, or not at all. That's a choice?

Whatever happened to leisure? It costs a lot, not the time but the equipment required to enjoy it, and the clothes deemed necessary to enjoy it, all part of lifestyle these days. I won't even discuss sports paraphernalia and the games people play. Just consider for a moment the humble picnic in the park. What began with egg and onion sandwiches and lemonade expanded to ham on rye and beer, segued into fried chicken and plonk wine, and evolved into focaccia with grilled veggies, goat cheese and radicchio salad, Mimosas and iced cappuccino. Lifestyle and money go hand to mouth.

No choice is simple anymore, if it ever was. It seems every choice we make has a price tag attached, and it's all to do with our lifestyle. Then as each item on our wish list comes true, another pops up like a duck (note the word duck; see ducks, p. 81) in a shooting gallery and we have another goal to shoot for. Every choice we make costs.

Whatever happened to savings? When did budget become a dirty word? Why isn't buying on time as easy as "they" say it is (see Media, p. 61)? We spend a lot of talk on lifestyle. Style sounds so cool, lots of pizzazz, lots of glamour. That's why it costs so much. Try some other phrases: life ways, life model, life patterns, life design, design for living – they all sound superficial, like something out of *Vanity Fair* or *People* magazine. Let's talk about priorities. What are yours? Now take your choice.

Don't you wish it were that simple? It's easy to say this lifestyle is just not it, not what you had in mind, and to wish things were different; but unless you can see how to change the locked-in pattern, you are going to be depressed. How can you change something when you feel so trapped?

Start simply. Ask yourself a few questions about your present lifestyle, your pleasures, your choices. Is there something you'd regret never doing again? Is there something else you don't care if you don't do again? Is there something you'd rather never have to do or face again? I'm sure you'll find there are people too, but they're harder to eliminate. For now, find something you can part with. Ease it out of your life. You'll feel better in the morning. I just want you to get the idea that your lifestyle does not own you.

Now a caution. Did you ever hear of sunset depression? I'm not a sailor but I understand that when people are sailing in some exotic waters and drench themselves with more beauty than they can assimilate, they get depressed. The first glorious sunset or sunrise is breathtaking and uplifting; the second is wonderful and makes you ask how can you be so lucky, so blessed; the third is yeah, wow, there it is again, isn't that nice; the fourth, they tell me, is depressing. Isn't it ever going to rain? Gardeners tell me that their first exquisite tiny new potatoes warm from the soil, barely steamed, are melt-in-the-mouth delicious, ditto tomatoes from their own vines. However, a plethora of potatoes and an embarrassment of tomatoes must be dealt with while you and your family have a finite number of mouths. So you parcel out the veggies to friends and neighbors, anyone who will take some off your hands and table. There's probably a psychological phrase for this ungrateful syndrome, because we all have it. The point is, you can't always trust your own indifference. You really like new potatoes; you really enjoy vine-ripened tomatoes. Don't do anything rash. Just consider your choices more carefully. One sunset too many does not justify a complete change of lifestyle.

The trouble may be that you're bored. You pick up an idea, add another wish to your list, and before you can add to your debt load, you find that someone else has been there, done that. Suddenly you're not so keen. This is something like being informed when you have just discovered a new Web site that 3,542 people have been there before you. You don't want to follow in anyone else's smeary snail trails. This is an inverse lifestyle syndrome and just as nasty as the straightforward gimme approach. I'm not sure which is less attractive: Me Too or Me First.

You really should figure out what you want before you get it and before it's too late.

You know that old story about the man who set his ladder against a very tall house and he climbed and he climbed and he climbed and when he got to the roof he discovered it was the wrong house. Don't you do that. If you're going to all the trouble of climbing you'd better be sure you want what's at the top. Be careful what you wish for. A lot of people want to change their lives not because they climbed the wrong ladder but because they're bored with the ladder they're on. Is all this effort worth it? Is that all there is? What are you going to do about it? As Nobel Prize winner Elias Canetti said (in a neat little journal of aphorisms and afterthoughts), "How simple it would be if God could help. My answer to that is, 'How do we know God hasn't?'"

It takes years to realize where you've been and what you've been doing. You hear people say, "I don't know what I thought I was doing"; or, "I can't think what got into me"; or, "What did I have in mind?" You've probably said it yourself. I have. At the time you're referring to, you probably thought you were fully conscious. You probably think you're fully conscious now. But unless you were blessed enough to be born damaged or different and did something about it (with help), most of your experience is probably still untouched; you may have lived through it but you aren't aware of it or of its lessons. You just did it. It's there, inside you somewhere, but you still don't know what to do with it. Look at it like part of a dormant vocabulary: you have a vague idea of what a word means but you've never used it in a sentence. Why not try?

See, before you can change your lifestyle you have to change your attitudes. Before you can change your attitudes you have to change your environment. That's why you're reading this book. You want to change your environment. You may think it's simplistic to do this by changing brands, venues, shopping habits, toothpaste, but it's the only way.

The late American genius Buckminster Fuller said that it was impossible to change human nature and almost as difficult to change behavior. What is necessary is to change the environment. Thus, if you're going to stop people from killing themselves driving, you build safer cars and you legislate seat belts.

I remember reading a science fiction story half a century ago so forgive me for not knowing who wrote it (someone will tell me). An astronaut has survived a crash onto another planet that destroyed his ship and killed the entire crew except him. This planet is almost user-friendly. There is oxygen but the air is thin and the man has to take deep breaths. The atmosphere is quite cold and a wind blows constantly, so he is grateful to find a shelter he can inhabit, though he has to crouch to enter. He finds water, of a sort, to wash in and though it's bitter, he can drink it. He finds food – again, not what he's used to, but he can eat it, keep it down and keep himself alive. So he lives. I'm making up details but I remember the end when it describes this man, who used to be a normal human being, as he showers and enjoys the sharp liquid sluicing over his carapace, turning the thick hair on his body into a wet mat which he enjoys scrubbing, taking deep breaths from his huge chest – and so on. He changed, you see, to adapt to his new environment. And so will you.

Still, we look longingly at people who we think have got everything. A lot of people, when asked what it would take to feel rich, used to say about $15,000 more than they're making, no matter what their income was. A recent survey indicates they would feel comfortable if they could only make twice what they're making now. Is wealth always beyond one's grasp? If you play your cards right, swing that deal, get that raise, win that lottery, then rich is what you'll be. How would you like to be truly rich? Your choice. Do you want to make a living or get a life?

Livelihood

No great improvements
in the lot of mankind are possible
until a great change takes place
in the fundamental constitution
of their modes of thought.
– J. S. Mill

Here's a questionnaire taken from the Winter 1993 issue of *Canadian Social Trends*, the quarterly magazine published by Statistics Canada, from the 1992 General Social Survey (GSS):

1. I plan to slow down in the coming year.
2. I consider myself a workaholic.
3. When I need more time, I tend to cut back on my sleep.
4. At the end of the day, I often feel that I have not accomplished what I set out to do.
5. I worry that I don't spend enough time with my family and friends.
6. I feel that I'm constantly under stress trying to accomplish more than I can handle.
7. I feel trapped in a daily routine.
8. I feel that I just don't have time for fun anymore.
9. I often feel under stress when I don't have enough time.
10. I would like to spend more time alone.

The writer of the accompanying article, Judith Frederick, comments on the results of the survey, saying that if you agree with four or more of the above statements, you should consider yourself "time-crunched, and in the company of almost one-half (45 percent) of Canadians aged 15 and over."

If you agree with seven or more then you, along with about 15 percent of all adult Canadians, are experiencing very high levels of time-crunch stress.

We all know what stress is. It's your body's way of telling you to simplify your life. Make your livelihood lively, not killing. Dr. Hans Selye, the late Dutch-born endocrinologist who we claim as Canadian, was way ahead of the current chatter about stress, which has everyone clucking about how bad it is for you and how you should simmer down, as in *downsize*, before it's too late. He dedicates his 1956 book, *The Stress of Life*, as follows:

> *This book is dedicated to those who are not afraid*
> *to enjoy the stress of a full life,*
> *nor too naive to think that they can do so*
> *without intellectual effort.*

The fact is that a certain amount of stress is good for you. On the physical level alone, you wouldn't develop muscles if you didn't subject them to stress, called exercise (or work). Dr. Selye relates the general adaptation syndrome (GAS), the method by which our various internal organs and nervous system enable us to adapt to change, to the broader adjustment that people must make to the individual circumstances of their lives. Life, Selye writes, is "largely a process of adaptation" and stress is the "rate of all the wear and tear caused by life."

No one can avoid stress but everyone can find ways to reduce it and to lessen its damaging side effects. One of the ways is *deviation* (Selye's term): step aside. Stop the world and get off. Find something else to do. Find an outlet. "Nothing," writes Selye, "erases unpleasant thoughts more effectively than conscious concentration on pleasant ones." We know *that*.

In my book *Family*, I commented on the fact that today's families, however differently they may be structured or defined, consider time spent together to be top priority. In a recent survey, workers revealed that they would be willing to cut their overtime work, hence pay, in order to spend more time with their families. Perhaps it's the influence of the women, that is, the wives and mothers, in the labor force, but fewer of them are willing to put their careers ahead of their families, and they are finally making this clear to employers. The conscious sacrifice of some families to return the working woman to the home, for at least as long as the children are preschool – but often longer – has been another manifestation of the desire for a simpler life. If you take a significant drop in income, then life must of necessity become simpler, that is, less expensive. It's an economic consequence. Thus, one's very livelihood gets caught up in the discussion about the quality of life.

Leo Buscaglia is not the only feel-good communicator who tells us how important hugs are. The late psychologist Virginia Satir had it down to a formula. She used to say you need four hugs a day to live, eight to maintain, and twelve to grow. I like the distinction between living, maintaining and growing. We all must make a living, and we want to find a livelihood that suits us for maintenance, but we aren't going to stop there. We want to keep on growing.

"Live Lightly on the Earth." That's the endearing catch phrase of another simple set – one of the communities multiplying like weeds and blooming like tulips in the springtime. It's getting so you have to tiptoe through the slogans, and memorize the acronyms. Still, Live Lightly is one of the better ones, quite poetic. What does it mean, exactly? It's quite ecological in its implications.

I went to the Galapagos Islands a few years ago, opting for a ten-passenger sailboat that could take us to the smaller, more ecologically vulnerable islands. A panga (a large rowboat with a motor) brought us to shore where we could wade onto a beach and explore. Even on the remoter islands, wooden stakes, although set widely apart, outlined the walkways, indicating where we must walk. Our guide pointed out a fuzzy footprint on the ground outside the path. We watched the wind gently lift a few grains of sand from the indentation as he told us that someone had strayed perhaps a month before, as he judged the soft, sand-brushed surface. Harm had been done.

That footprint in the sand is my metaphor for living lightly, both metaphor and warning. No matter how lightly we step, we leave a mark, and do not know the harm we do. If we're going to live more simply, we must take care where we step, earning our right to walk the paths. Live lightly, one step at a time. We'll figure out how to keep you in sneakers, and on the trail. We all have to make a living; living is the means to an end. Livelihood is the way, that path we must be so careful with, doing no harm.

"What do you want to be when you grow up?" Remember that question? And kids still say an astronaut, a doctor, a teacher, a fireman, a nurse, a writer. I know of one kid, son of a friend of mine, who said millionaire and was disappointed, when he looked it up in the encyclopedia, that there was no job description. I was a new girl in high school when the teacher asked that question aloud, going round the room, and everyone guffawed when I said mother. I thought the teacher meant what are you going to be and I was realistic enough to know that, whatever else, that would be my most likely occupation. What I really wanted was to be a writer – no, what I wanted was to write. Big difference.

It is seldom granted that we can so readily and arbitrarily choose what we're going to be, what we're going to do, as seems to be expected when we're very young. Girls, particularly – in my day certainly – grow up to a certain point with hopes and expectations and then suddenly, no matter how smart they are, realize the world has closed in and they don't have much choice. They must toe the gender line. Below a certain economic level, everyone runs into a brick wall that flattens possibility. You think that maybe today possibilities have opened up a little, but female hopefuls still bump their heads on glass ceilings and both genders blunt their dreams on other barriers, mostly financial.

Tinker, tailor, soldier, sailor, rich man, poor man, beggar man, thief. The occupations in that old choosing game bear scarcely any resemblance to what people do today. They would require a great deal of explanation and adaptation to make sense in today's economy. Simple as we want to become, these categories are too simple by far for us – except maybe thief. (The definition and job description are still similar.) As for housewife, Marilyn Waring and feminists around the world have been fighting that tag for decades; it's finally off the Canadian census questionnaire as an occupation.

Most of us still tend to identify ourselves by what we do. Catch phrases file us in others' memories as we do our best to make ourselves sound good:

- I'm in food management (waitress)
- I'm in circulation (paper boy/girl)
- I'm in sales (door-to-door peddler)
- I'm in communications (phone solicitor)
- I'm in direct mail (junk mail delivery person)
- I'm in domestic engineering (housewife).

The fact is that, romanticize or aggrandize it as we will, work defines us. We depend on work to give us an identity as well as a living. Most of us think we're worth more than we're being paid, that is, if we're lucky enough to be paid, and we fuss about the benefits. Most of us long for holidays or vacations, but most of us would be bored out of our skulls if we had too much free time on our hands, witness all those restless lottery winners. The work ethic still has us by the throat. Believe it or not, most people like to work. Just not all the time.

Have you seen those comparisons accountants come up with once in a while, estimating how many hours you'd have to work for a pair of shoes or an airline ticket in 1960 compared to the present day? There are lots of hidden agendas in these lists, designed subliminally to show you (a) how your dollars have shrunk in purchasing power; (b) how lucky you are to be able to afford shoes; (c) what a bargain you're getting in travel. Some of these comparisons include work-time estimates for Russia or for Third World countries and the rather odious revelations are designed to make you feel (a) grateful; and (b) guilty for complaining.

In their bestselling book, *Your Money or Your Life*, Joe Dominguez and Vicki Robin developed that work-time idea into a complete system. Their line, oft repeated, is "Money is something we choose to trade our life energy for." Life energy is another phrase for vitality, vital force, the power to live.

I still remember when one of my daughters began working, selling lottery tickets in a booth all day, and I kept thinking of her there, trapped by

LIFESTYLES AND LIVELIHOOD – **59**

her agreement, imprisoned by her desire for the payoff. I had never thought of anything I did in just those terms. I guess I'm a slow learner. I realized only then that this was the beginning of her life's tradeoff: selling time and energy for money. In the case of a stay-at-home mother, it's bartering time and energy for love, but it saves money. It's amazing what we will do for love or money.

"You've heard money talking," said the Canadian communications pundit Marshall McLuhan. "Did you understand the message?" The message now is the medium – money, a mutually agreed-upon medium of exchange. What Dominguez and Robin have done is raise our consciousness as to how much our tacit consent costs. We're back to the question of where your heart is, for there also is your money. I mention it here in a section on livelihood because, as I said, work tends to define us even as we identify ourselves with work. As Dominguez and Robin have indicated, what you do, how you live and what you spend your money on, depends on what those things mean to you, how much you want them, and what else you're buying along with them. In short, your choices are determined by your value system. Values are part of livelihood, more friendly to talk about than your life-energy, but they cost the same.

We each have our own particular value system. People spend a lot of money on things, which, to them, are expressions of themselves – their fastidious taste, their generosity or frugality, their artistic nature, their fears, their hidden desires – but which to others are just things. No accounting for tastes. Most of the time they are unaware, themselves, of what they're trying to buy besides another pair of shoes or a new CD or imported Belgian waffles or a book or a lottery ticket. Without analyzing our expenditures too closely, we can justify practically anything. Most of us consider ourselves careful, informed shoppers, even if we're not. After all, we know what we're doing, don't we? If we do, there's a credibility gap in most of us.

In 1995 the Merck Family Fund in the United States commissioned The Harwood Group, a research firm, to study people's perspectives on consumption. The study began with four focus groups in different regions of the United States and then, informed by the concerns raised in the focus groups, moved on to a national public opinion survey. Much like the similar Decima (Canadian research group) survey conducted in Canada ten years earlier, the findings revealed a gap between what consumers were doing in the marketplace and what a majority of them said they would be satisfied with. Over 66 percent of those surveyed said they would be much more satisfied if they were able to spend more time with family and friends; much happier (56 percent) if there were less stress in their lives, and much more pleased (56 percent) if they felt what they were doing made a difference. Many people described the treadmill feeling, running for material goods that seemed forever harder to reach. Some questioned this perpetual striving, wondering whether it was necessary to push so hard, or whether it was even a conscious choice to do so. They all blamed the Joneses. Keeping up with them was never so hard. "The Joneses are killing me," said one man.

They say they don't want merely to make a living, they want a life. Tell me what you believe in. Show me your value system. Put your money where your mouth is, for there also is your heart. What kind of person would you like to be? It costs a lot to be human.

5

Media and the Cultural Environment

TV is not so much an action,
as a re-action, medium.
– Marshall McLuhan

Media is plural. I cut my wisdom teeth on Marshall McLuhan and I know perfectly well that the medium is the message. When I am bombarded by the media, I try to hide. I wonder what the late, great communications guru would say about the message we are getting now, and its widespread, devastating effects. The message is *to consume*.

The theory behind consumer demand is two-fold. First, wants continue to be urgent even as they seem to be satisfied. That's something the media count on. Even when people have enough, something else is missing. The late American psychologist Abraham Maslow theorized that after people's physical needs are met (food, shelter, safety), they start searching for fulfillment, a psychological desire that will never be entirely met – at least, not noticeably. The second aspect is that "want" is in the appetite of the consumer – never mind why or where it originates. It's the huckster's job, as he sees it, to whet both the psychological desires and the physical wants of the consumer. The idea of satiation is incomprehensible. Since when is enough enough? Just keep everything coming on down the (assembly) line.

The really neat thing about this, from the seller's point of view, is that items like bread or water that everybody needs are relatively cheap while frivolous things like diamonds that nobody needs are very expensive. It's up to the advertiser to create the demand for useless, exotic, playful self-indulgences. John Kenneth Galbraith explains all this succinctly in his book *The Affluent Society*. He concludes, wryly, that "economic theory has managed to transfer the sense of urgency in meeting consumer need that once was felt in a world where more production meant more food for the hungry, more clothing for the cold, and more houses for the homeless, to a world where increased output satisfies the craving for more elegant automobiles, more exotic food, more erotic clothing, more elaborate entertainment – indeed for the entire modern range of sensuous, edifying, and lethal desires." (Hold that word *lethal.*) Keep those Rollses rolling! We all become victims of our own desires, manipulated by the people who put them there.

Dr. George Gerbner, professor of communications at the University of Pennsylvania and founder of the Cultural Environment Movement, says you don't have take over the military or change legislation to control a nation; all you have to do is control the storyteller. Television is the storyteller. Our saving grace may be that people are finding it harder and harder to believe – especially the commercials, and now, the news. Duane Elgin, the most recent founding father of the simple living movement, who brought Gerbner to my attention, says that we're all going slightly schizophrenic on this, "on the one hand knowing we need to learn to live with less, and on the other hand being continuously encouraged to consume ever more." We seem to be unable not to believe the claims we claim not to believe. We keep on consuming.

For one thing, we all eat too much. "Living with televison means growing up in a world of about 22,000 commercials a year, 5,000 of them for food products, more than half of which are for low-nutrition sweets and snacks."[1] And yet, even while we eat, we are aware of the following (only the exact figures may be unfamiliar):

- 20 years ago fashion models weighed 8 percent less than the average female. Today, models weigh 23 percent less than the average female.

- 80 percent of 10-year-old girls diet.
- 8 million Americans suffer from anorexia or bulimia.
- 11 percent of female college students suffer from bulimia nervosa.
- 70 percent of normal weight women want to be thinner.
- 23 percent of underweight women think they are overweight.
- 72 percent of women will be on a diet in any given year.
- 50 percent of middle-aged women identify their weight as the most important thing they would like to change in their lives.
- 11- to 17-year-old girls' number one magic wish is to be thinner.[2]

Where do you think they got the idea that they were too fat? Never mind that it's a man's world, the media works both sides of the shopping aisle, telling us on one side of their mouths that we deserve a break today and on the other that females have to be thin to be acceptable.

What other media messages lodge in the mind? Lodge? They take up permanent residency and change the decorating. Little kids give concerts for their families and for visiting relatives at Christmas/festive times, just as they always have, only now they sing commercial jingles they have picked up from the box. Grownups get teary-eyed and nostalgic when they hum or sing or try to piece together the words of a jingle or the theme song of a favorite sitcom when they were kids. Television has furnished us with an entire new mythology and folklore.

I used to give creative writing workshops in the schools, a grueling source of grocery money funded by the Ontario Arts Council for struggling poets, playwrights and writers. I often staged an improv: pulling students up on their feet to ad lib their way through an existing story to show them how scene development and dialogue worked. I discovered that the hardest part was finding a classic story they all knew, with equal time for male and female protagonists. I chose *Hansel and Gretel*. Then, before we started, I would go around the room getting each person to tell me part of the story to make sure it was familiar to all of them. Later, in the hopes that some might actually know the story, I would ask the teacher ahead of time to assign it to her pupils as preparatory reading. When that didn't work, I asked the teacher to *tell* her kids the story ahead of time. Always, I had to fill in the blanks of an alien tale before we could begin to act it out.

On the other hand, once I was asked to help the students (Grade 7–8) write a character sketch of a well-known storybook heroine. They chose "Pretty Woman" because they all knew who she was, having seen the movie. So it was Cinderella, sort of, or Sleeping Beauty, anyway, the hooker with a heart of gold who got the Prince in the end. Where once people had a basic knowledge of Greek mythology and fairy tales – Anderson and Grimm – now all they have are commercials and Disney. That's kids, you say. Adults know better, know more than that. How can they?

Newspapers and television news are giving us the same kind of fairy tales. Telling stories has become a necessary political skill, perhaps even diplomatic. Hard-hitting journalists, in their need to be liked and to be read, soften their blows and reduce their in-depth studies to quick, palatable bites for instant consumption. Yet side-by-side with the toothless editorial are the claws and fangs of the news. By this time we all know the formula for the lead story: "If it bleeds, it leads."

Our tendency is to think in story lines and the media indulge our wishes. Story is what we all crave, ever since people gathered around the fire in the cave and listened to the histories of their ancestors and the tales of the hunt. We're all still waiting for the punch line. Will it be the boffo laugh-getter or the happily-ever-after sop or the comforting reassurance that such horror stories will never happen to you? Whoever tells us the best story wins – not the tellers, not the tales, but the sponsors – and they win big. The audience, wherever it is, whoever they are, know the names, know the products, know what they want to buy, and if they don't have the money, they think about how to get it. Vulnerable and bloodthirsty, they soak up a homogeneous cultural environment that transcends national differences. Canadian sci-fi writer William Gibson, who gave us the word *cyberspace*, thinks that in the future people will be identified more by the products they consume or crave than by their ethnic or cultural connections. Disney versus The Little Mermaid? That future is already here, and people are killing for it.

The worst of it is, violence is cheaper to produce and requires no translation. It travels well. The common denominator is blood. Everyone bleeds. Advertisers get an immediate return on their investment. It's estimated that 50 percent of US media income comes from abroad. Would you call this blood money?

Now consider these statistics.

- At the height of its popularity, *Power Rangers* was seen by 300 million children every night: Martial Arts for the teenyboppers, considered okay because at the end of a half-hour of violence someone cautioned kids not to act like that.
- Five murders per hour occur in prime time, and that's just the news!
- In 1980, the most violent prime-time TV show registered 22 acts of violence per hour; in 1992 the most violent prime-time show registered 60 acts of violence per hour.[3]
- There are at least three "entertainment" murders a night.
- Cartoons have 20 to 25 violent incidents an hour. Another source rates them at 80 to 100 per hour.
- By the time a child reaches adolescence, he (more likely he) will have seen 18,000 violent deaths on the box.
- According to a Canadian report, by the age of 12 a child will have seen up to 12,000 acts of violence: murder, rape, assaults and all those nasty things that give kids nightmares (until they get used to them?).[4]
- Over 1,000 studies conclude that exposure to TV violence increases the likelihood of aggressive behavior, especially in males. (The fact is that girls don't watch as much, and watch different things.)

All the surveys, after initial divided conclusions, are increasingly in agreement as to the effects of witnessed violence on young minds and developing behavior patterns.

Dr. Gerbner is among the most articulate critics of the 20th-century culture of violence, the one who coined the phrase "*the mean street syndrome*" to identify the effect of all this random "entertaining" brutality, from which there seems to be no protection. He says that "the TV environment is a major transformation in the socialization of the species, emanating from a (shrinking) handful of global conglomerates with something to sell. The people in charge of this are *not even media people.*[5] (Italics mine.) That's the scary part.

The Cultural Environment Movement (CEM) was founded in St. Louis in March 1996, by 250 concerned citizens who share the following objectives:

- liberating creative people from the formulas imposed on them
- creating more jobs to give newcomers (ideas?) a chance
- protecting creative opportunities
- refuting the system in which we are all trapped
- creating a better cultural environment for our children.

CEM has a strong Canadian component, evident in the Pre-Convention Summit on International Broadcast Standards it helped bring about. Canadian speakers included Keith Spicer, then Chair of the Canadian Radio-Television and Telcommunications Commission; Ron Cohen, Chair, Canadian Broadcast Standards Council; and Marc Raboy, Professor of Communications, University of Montreal, plus other panel participants from Great Britain, France, South Africa, Croatia, Germany and the United States. George Gerbner addressed the group, reminding them that they were asembled to achieve the impossible.

"We are in a new age," he said. "We have to realize that this new globalized, conglomeratized, standardized cultural environment is damaging to our children, our democracy, society and communities."

The media, specifically the entertainment industry, claim it is impossible to set any unviersal standards because of the global nature of new technologies, but Gerbner points out that the world already lives within strict international broadcast standards. The only trouble is, he points out, that these standards are defined by a few men in Hollywood. When these people argue that they're only presenting "reality," Gerbner shows them research (from his 15-year study) with revealing statistics about prime-time TV. For example, men outnumber women three to one; there are significantly smaller proportions of young people, old people, blacks, Hispanics, and other minorities on television than in the US population at large, while crime is at least ten times as prevalent on TV as in the real world.

Richard Gregg, the Quaker who preceded Duane Elgin in his espousal of voluntary simplicity, said that for those who believe in nonviolence, simplicity is essential. He states it baldly (simply?): *Simplicity helps to prevent violence.* The reason is simple: people who live simply have nothing to lose. They can afford to stand up and be counted, because that's all there is to count. Not only that, their behavior will make a difference (count) because they will be seen to be sincere. They mean what they say.

You've heard the expression, "put your money where your mouth is," meaning, if you really believe what you are saying, back up your words with money, go ahead and bet on them. For people who have no money but who believe in their cause, the challenge should read: "Put your life where your mouth is." The meaning of life does not lie in the value of what we consume; satisfaction is not to be had from over-consumption; identity does not depend on a brand name the media have turned into a household word; redemption does not consist of the bad guy getting caught. If McLuhan were alive today, he'd turn over in his grave.

6

The Fisherman's Wife and Feminism

Women want men, careers, money, children,
friends, luxury, comfort, independence,
freedom, respect, love
and three-dollar pantyhose that won't run.
– Phyllis Diller

Remember the fisherman's wife? Never satisfied, always wanted more more more. Pity the poor old fella, her husband, out fishing every day, catching scarcely enough to keep body and soul together, living in a miserable hovel. So one day he catches a talking fish. Not only does the fish talk, it offers him anything his heart desires if he'll toss it back. Why not? Probably tough, anyway, has to be pretty old, must take time for a fish to learn to talk. That night the man has something new to tell his wife. Guess what happened today? You'll never believe it.

She believes it. And wants whatever the fish has to offer.

"Go back," she says to her husband. "And ask for a decent house to live in." He doesn't know how hard it is, sitting in a hovel all day, not that she sits that much, there's always work to be done, even around a hovel.

So the fisherman goes back, hollers for the fish and tells it what he wants.

"It's not me," he says. "It's the wife. She'd like a nice house."

"No problem," says the fish.

And so it goes, from hovel to house to mansion to castle to how about Queen of the World? Too much.

"That's it," says the fish. "Go back where you started from and don't bother me again."

So the fisherman goes back to his hovel and his wife, the woman who couldn't be satisfied. And did they live happily ever after? At least they had a lot to talk about.

I think this story is supposed to illustrate the consequences of greed, of asking for too much, and, of course, that it's all the woman's fault for never being content. Maybe the moral is "quit while you're ahead." The husband would have been happy in a nice house. As for that, he wasn't complaining in his hovel. It was all her big ideas that led them up and then down again, to rot there on the beach and mutter "if only" for the rest of their lives. Happily ever after.

The story is about greed, yes, and also about ego and pride and hunger. Don't underestimate hunger. It has been my observation that people who grow up hungry will never have enough to eat, a corollary of their attitude to money. Psychic hunger doesn't go away; it's lifelong and it's going to emerge later, often in antisocial ways. I wish our politicians and governments would remember that as they slash welfare payments; I wish divorced fathers would remember that as they welsh on child support payments. I wish we could all keep that firmly in mind every time we pass a food bank pickup box. We must not forget the children, the future generation.

But what about women? What about the fisherman's wife? What about her greed and her hunger, her pride and her ego? There isn't enough money in the world to satisfy her, not even from a magic fish. What kind of role model is she for the cause of feminism today? How does she fit into the ideal of the simple life? What would Marilyn Waring say?

Marilyn Waring, as everyone knows by now, is a New Zealand activist, the young MP (youngest ever to be elected to Parliament) who cast the deciding vote to make her country nuclear-free. A professor of social policy and a farmer, Waring is a social change agent encouraging women every-where in the world to put a price on their unpaid labor and trying to per-suade governments to take it into account in their estimates of the Gross Domestic Product (GDP). She's the one ultimately responsible for the changes in Canada's census categories and questions. A Canadian woman, like a Canadian man, can now call herself "householder," and can (in a random ten-minute questionnaire) report the number of hours of unpaid labor she performs. Eventually someone is going to count them.

Waring's bestselling book *If Women Counted: A New Feminist Econom-ics*[1] has caused revolutionary thinking in women around the world since it was published in 1990. In 1995, the National Film Board released the film *Who's Counting?*, a full-length documentary of a world tour Waring made, investigating and lecturing about the economic value of women's unpaid work. Her third book, *Three Masquerades: Essays on Equality, Work and Hu-man Rights*, was published in New Zealand in 1996 and in Canada and the United States in 1997. In it she documents the inequities of women's treat-ment in the political world, the invisibility of their unpaid labor, and their lack of protection and safeguards under international human rights con-ventions. These inequities can't help but make you wonder about the value of a "simple life" to a woman. How can women be content with less when so few of them have ever had more?

The remarkable fact is that women are way ahead of the men in their drive for the simple life. Their participation, according to Duane Elgin, outnumbers men two to one. The qualities they espouse are traits that are usually assigned to women: compassion, concern, nurturance, frugality and so on. Most of the simple living handbooks ignore the political aspect of the GDP entirely, and I'm going to have to as well, especially when we get to the frugal tips and homely how-tos. Let's face it: this book is never going to be read in Nepal. Don't mention my name in Somalia. (I am reminded of a scene in the NFB film about Waring, when she is interviewing, through an interpreter, a group of women somewhere in Africa. She has just asked how much the men help with the feeding of the children – that is, with the gardening and gathering necessary to provide food for the family. She doesn't have to wait for the interpreter's reply. The answer is laughter. What – men help?)

The inner life recommended for North American women in the current spate of sweet, soft, abundantly simple books cannot be achieved merely by dabbing your light bulbs with aromatic oil, having a long hot bubble bath, or getting up an hour early to commune with your daily journal in order to maintain your serenity. Nor does cutting back on the book clubs, getting out the crock pot, making your own Christmas cards and doing your mending really entitle you to any awards for being conscientious. (It would be too stressful to consider competing for Woman of the Year or Woman of Achievement, wouldn't it?) Certainly there are lots of cute, fun things to do to qualify you as a simplicity expert, but these are all external things, having to do with ego and not with self.

Jacob Needleman refers to the fisherman's wife in *Money and the Meaning of Life*. In the book his enlightened businessman (something like a Jungian mentor) interprets the story as being about the need to know what one wants. He thinks that greed is inevitable in the absence of an inner aim. His idea is that if the inner life is fulfilled, greed/money loses its hold. "Happily ever after," he says, "is fairy-tale language for the state of inner freedom, freedom from the illusions of the ego." To gain such freedom it is necessary to want something beyond what ego alone can fulfill but to which the ego can assent. My guess is that he means the simple life, the real fairy tale – "a new morality," he calls it, whereby we learn to love "as we have heard of love in the teachings of the masters. This world," Needleman concludes, "becomes my monastery."

So what happens to women? "Get thee to a nunnery, go!"

Many of the values and lifestyles espoused by the simple living movement have been identified in other times and contexts as feminine. Nurturing, caregiving, centering in the home, creating simple abundance, are all soft, loving activities women have been associated with over the centuries. Women were the midwives long before men picked up their forceps and elbowed them out of the way; women reared and educated the children, not to forget that they bore them in the first place; women baked the bread and brewed the ale; they nursed the sick and laid out the dead. Over the years their work load and respect have been diminished by paid professionals and their responsibility effectively removed. Now they're not even supposed to be the consumers they were trained to be in the 19th and first half of the 20th centuries. More correctly, they're expected now to cut expenses while drastically changing their patterns of consumption in deference to the ecological crisis the world is facing. What else can they do but be simple?

Duane Elgin (*Voluntary Simplicity*) says that "to live with simplicity is to unburden our lives – to live more lightly, cleanly, aerodynamically [aerodynamically!]..." It's a way of life that everyone must decide for herself, he acknowledges, not a path of "no growth" but a way of "new growth" – with a spiritual dimension.

This kind of simplicity is not, Elgin emphasizes, just another name for poverty. I'm happy to learn that, because North American poverty can't begin to touch the Third World for deprivation and hardship. Poverty in itself will not make voluntary simplicity work. "It is," says Elgin, "a more demanding intention of living with balance." Women are good at that. They've had a lot of practice.

Several years ago I wanted to write a book called "The Balancing Act," but I couldn't interest a publisher. Someone else published a book of that name, more of a financial text than I had envisioned. I bring it up now because I found the outline for my phantom book, and some of my ideas seem to apply to women today who are attempting to live in voluntary simplicity. Here's a quiz from Section Three designed to raise a woman's consciousness to an awareness of herself:

- If you're so efficient why don't you ever have any time?
- If you have it all why are you complaining?
- If you're such a superhuman being why are you being ignored?
- If you're such a good daughter why does your mother keep telling you you're not? (Blood is thicker than water but sometimes you wish it weren't.)

- If you're so great in bed why is your Significant Other having an affair with someone else?
- And what does your Significant Other see in that bosomy airhead who doesn't know Captain Nemo from a Nautilus?
- If you're such a good cook why is your family addicted to peanut butter?
- What would you do without take-out?
- If you're so fit why do you find it so hard to get out of bed in the morning?
- If you're so smart about money why aren't you rich?
- If you're so conscientious why aren't you perfect?
- If you're so perfect why aren't you happy?
- Whose fault is it, anyway?

Pretty depressing, actually. I guess I can understand why the publisher gave it a pass. But these are the kinds of questions you're supposed to be asking yourself now before you stop fussing and scale down.

The American novelist Erica Jong said that you don't have to beat a woman if you can make her feel guilty. The voluntary simplicity movement is almost guaranteed to make a woman feel guilty as she sees how far she falls short of this "beauty and functional integrity that elevates our lives" (Duane Elgin's description). In the outline of my book-that-never-was, I was going to identify some of the sources of guilt that women have to cope with:

- performance guilt (addiction to perfection)
- expectations guilt (never enough)
- emotional/psychological guilt (nice girls don't get angry)
- ethical guilt (whatever became of sin?).

As for my solutions – how to feel good in spite of feeling guilty – I was going to explain that guilt, like love, is holistic, and the way to treat it is holistically. Obviously, I was ahead of my time. The ways I was going to suggest achieving this are as follows. Pay close attention because they are Everywoman's Guide to the Simple Life:

- change your expectations
- reset your goals

- establish your priorities
- be good to yourself
- make your wants known
- laugh
- cry
- forgive
- forget
- talk
- listen.

(The moral is, never throw away a file!)

So here we are, back on the feminist trail, attempting inner growth and upward spirituality while remembering to clean the windows with environmentally friendly vinegar. The menfolk are finding voluntary simplicity much more interesting and challenging because they're out there creating a whole new currency. O Brave New World! As for us fishwives, we're just making do with the old: making one dollar do the work of two and trying not to damage the ozone layer. Woman's work is never done. Sigh.

7

Saving the Environment

*An enduring environmental ethic will aim
to preserve not only the health and freedom
of our species, but access to the world
in which the human spirit was born.*
– Edward O. Wilson

During World War II it was a patriotic duty on the part of Canadians to salvage usable material from what would have been garbage in order for it to be recycled for the war effort. People poured bacon drippings into fat cans to be saved for something to do with guns, I think. (There were jokes about that: "Ladies, bring your fat cans to the Salvage Depot!" I was so young my brother had to explain it to me.) People wound bits of string or wadded foil into mammoth balls, and saved paper and any reusable metals. Every city had regular Salvage Days when people put their recyclable materials out on the street for pickup. Everyone gave away their treasures, like ornamental wrought-iron gates and fences. It was the patriotic thing to do.

The first patriotic thing I had to do was in a school sewing class when I had to take apart a pair of my father's civilian trousers and turn them into a skirt. I hated it. Maybe that's why I never learned to sew. As a patriotic, also frugal, gesture I wore hand-me-downs from an aunt who joined the

Canadian Women's Army Corps (CWAC). A poster with a rhyming slogan reminded civilians of what they could do for the war effort:

Use it up
Wear it out
Make it do
Do without.

Fifty years later we've finally come back to the idea of recycling so-called waste material as we realize how important it is not to squander the planet's resources. The corollary to that little WWII jingle is expressed even more simply today in the 4Rs:

Reduce
Reuse
Recycle
Recover.

Environment Canada recommends we incorporate these into our daily routine. Blue Boxes are scattered around the country taking over where the Salvage Corps left off, declaring Your City Recycles. And if people don't Recycle, then they owe it to themselves and to the planet to perform the other services – Reduce, Reuse, and Recover – even those they'd rather forget about because they're too much bother to have anything to do with. Those 4Rs are yet another source of guilt. They make you think uneasily about things you never thought about.

I have never consciously purchased an rubber band in my life, yet I have this compulsion now to save them when I receive them. I do use one occasionally, to keep the covers of a paperback from curling, or to batten down my check book when the bills are bulging out of it – such a good reason for direct withdrawal! Some people are very fond of rubber bands; postal workers and broccoli packagers come to mind, and Hilary Knight's character Eloise, who likes to wrap one around the end of her nose.

As for paper clips, I must admit I do buy them and use them a lot. Recently, fearing that I was running out, I bought an Armageddon-sized economy package of 12 boxes of paper clips, 100 per box. Ridiculous. If there is an Armageddon, there won't be any paper to clip.

Then I cleaned out my desk drawers and discovered that my fear of a dearth of paper clips was unfounded. There were 349 clips at large in my desk. I also have so many rubber bands they stretch my imagination. How can anyone eat that much broccoli? I used three thick rubber bands to anchor the heavy cord on an obsolete surge protector, stuffed the rest into a plastic bag and sealed it with a twistum. I never seem to have enough twistums.

This is serious. This is about plethora and overage and conspicuous consumption and pollution and ecology. We all own too much and use too little of it at the same time as we squander other things and accumulate constantly. If you don't have a guilty conscience about paper clips, take a guess at how many safety pins are lurking in your house. How many emery boards do you own, or nail clippers, keychains, stick pens, bottle openers, wine corks, calendars, notepads, empty yoghurt containers or pencil sharpeners? Of the latter, I found I had one blue, one red, one eyeliner sharpener, one swan, and two ducks (see ducks, p. 81). How is it, then, that I can never find a sharp pencil when I need one?

If you're a woman, how much bath gel do you own; if a man, how many bottles of aftershave lotion? These are not your fault; you never bought them. Don't you wonder sometimes, who does? Who actually buys scented drawer liners and exploding golf balls and plug-in, light-up air fresheners and multichopper kitchen gadgets and plastic bottle shapes to fit on drink cans? You never have. I never have. It's not our fault. But then, most things are not our fault. Things just have a way of piling up. We must learn to be watchful before such accumulation threatens to take over our lives, vigilant not only about the threat of conspicuous consumption but also about the rearguard attack of feverish frugality, which brings its own cumulative purgatory with it.

I knew of a man who carefully folded and saved every brown paper liquor bag he ever received, plus all the wine corks. He left this legacy to a friend I helped move into the man's vacated apartment. I know someone who saves bread wrappers, crumbs and all. I have a friend who reuses sticky notes, which is very conscientious, but what a clutter! These are borderline nut cases, you say; you don't ever do that. Where does frugality stop and compulsion begin, not to say madness? Look at the Collyer brothers.

For those too young to remember, the Collyer brothers were New York recluses who were discovered dead in the 1950s, trapped in the burrow of their Park Avenue home amidst a literal maze of newspapers and the accumulation of a lifetime, including a Stutz Bearcat in the living room. They had never thrown away a thing. I know of one novel (by Marcia Davenport) and one play (by an unknown playwright, trying out in summer stock in Westport, Connecticut) about the Collyer brothers. All very well to write about them, but imagine living like that! I have always held their example before me when too many things, especially paper, threaten to take over my world, or at least, usurp my drawers and cupboards.

Spring is a lovely time to clean out one's drawers and conscience. I started the habit when I was an undergraduate, performing an act of attrition when I finished my exams. Clearing out things was a metaphor for the clearing process going on in my brain. Just before my last exam in my fourth year, I made a bet with a friend I used to have coffee with, that I would indeed clean out my desk drawers. To prove it when I did, I sent him seven discarded items, one from each drawer. I won, and he took me to a movie. The only trouble was, I married him a few years later and it turned out he was a packrat and he still had those seven items, so they came back into my purlieu. I think that may be a cautionary tale, though it had a happy ending.

As I have told you, I got rid of most of my possessions in order to squeeze down into this cottage I'm living in now. But possessions, even after one has been very stern and ascetic about them, have a way of piling up again. Just as life is what happens when you are doing something else, so possessions are what creep in before this petty pace is over. By the time I moved in here I was light-headed, fancy-free, and almost footloose. But now I have a lot of paper clips and far too many ducks.

Let my ducks be an object lesson to all those who think that once they have cleared out their closets and dumped their detritus they are forever free. There I was, swept clean of ornaments and paintings and gewgaws, as well as bibelots and trinkets and *tchotchkes* (there's a word for them in every language). I wanted only one thing, one piece of art, specifically, a sculpture by a friend whose work in welded steel, I feared, would soon pass beyond my price range. (It has.) Hilary Cole gave me a deal on one of her smaller sculptures – a duck. My prototype duck still sits on a shelf, scarcely noticed by my grandchildren who make it their business when they visit to count my ducks.

The next duck floated to me on a paper pond, a small flotilla comprising mama duck and three babies with bodies made of a single pussy willow bud. The pond is encircled in paper, suspended on a thread, and attached by suction cup to a window. I bought it because I thought it would deter the birds from concussing themselves on the window behind their feeder. Other such Guard Ducks followed, bought to save the birds and not to satisfy my acquisitive nature. The basket ducks came next, from small to smallest, useful for storing small items in the bathroom. Or perhaps the duck magnets swam ahead of them, sailing across my fridge door, anchoring the pictures of my grandchildren and my recipes. By that time, I had made a rule: all ducks had to be functional. Because also by that time, people were giving me ducks and I wanted to avoid being the recipient, ever, of a decoy. Not that decoys aren't useful, but in a marsh, not on my coffee table. Besides, I have no space. As it is, I have duck sheets and pillowcases, comforter and curtains (in the Duck Room), a duck doorstop, duckorated light switch plate covers, duck tea towels and duck towel hangers, toilet brush, and paper towel dispenser, five duck letter openers, two duck pencil sharpeners (see above), a duck tape dispenser (a treasure, which I blackmailed a friend into giving me), a duck bellows, and a door-quacker. I retired the duck phone because every time it quacked (instead of ringing), my oldest grandson, when on the premises, would shout, "Shoot it! Shoot it!"

The point is, that even when you simplify your life, simplicity doesn't last. You have to keep on simplifying, keep on saying no, keep on shoving stuff out the door faster than you bring it in. No one ever said it was easy. It takes constant vigilance.

Environment Canada offers practical advice on its Web site to suggest ways of following the 4Rs. Here are a few of them:

- When you shop, try to find products that have little or no packaging.
- Repair your old appliances (if you can!) rather than buying new ones.
- Reuse jars, tins, and plastic tubs to store leftovers, bulk food and household items.
- But let me add a caution here: do not store poisonous or dangerous liquids (turpentine, insecticide, etc.) in deceptive containers. There is too much danger of a child drinking something harmful from a juice bottle.
- Buy good-quality, durable products that will last longer than sleaze.
- Help recycling along by buying recycled or recyclable products.
- Do a little recycling yourself. The crafts magazines are full of ideas for gifts or toys you can make with discards. There's a boutique in the Children's Museum in Boston which sells nothing but recyclable stuff – absolutely delectable, great for projects. If you don't use this stuff yourself, give it to an elementary school teacher you know. As education grants are being cut, art supplies and project materials will be among the first to vanish.
- At any store you shop at, ask yourself: can I reuse or recycle the packaging on this product? Was it made from recycled materials? In other words,
- Think before you buy.

Environment Canada gets pretty gruesome in its details. Did you know that landfill sites account for about 38 percent of Canada's total methane emissions? Methane is 20 times more potent as a greenhouse gas than carbon dioxide. Did you know that about one-third of our waste is paper and paperboard while another third is yard and kitchen waste? The remaining third is divided among long-lasting glass, metals, plastics, textiles, wood and other materials. Our garbage is very well made. Future archaeologists will marvel at it.

Here's an Environment Canada list of reductions you can make (I've even included their use of boldface):

Avoid food packaged in individual servings.

Buy in bulk. It saves money and the environment. [Forget this if you live alone.]

Buy multi-use items rather than single-use when possible.

Use your own cloth bags for shopping.

Donate your old clothes to charity.

Buy beverages in refillable containers.

Use rechargeable batteries.

Share your newspaper, magazines and books with a friend.

Wrap presents in reusable cloth bags or reused wrapping paper [or, I have read elsewhere, in the colored comic pages].

Rent [or borrow?] items you use infrequently.

Compost! [Unless you have, as I do, bears in the vicinity.]

Use both sides of every sheet of paper.[1] [This is my favorite. I save every letter or set of minutes I receive that's blank on the back. Very good for first drafts.]

Use a durable refillable mug or glass at school or work.

Encourage your friends and family to follow your good example. [If they can stand you.]

Be creative. This is like thinking of 100 uses for a dead cat. Maybe you can sell your bright ideas.

Think of something else you can do about reducing wastes.

The book produced by the Greater Vancouver Regional District, *101 Ways to Reuse your Old Shoes 'N Other Stuff*, is obviously dedicated to waste control and worth checking out. The copy is divided into two parts.

"Reuse Tips" describes reuse ideas and opportunities for clothing, appliances, musical instruments, home computers, toys, books, tapes and compact discs, furniture, home building and decorating materials, garden tools and sports equipment. It also explains how to reuse items such as old shower curtains and aluminium pie plates, how to wrap gifts creatively with reusable wrapping (done that), and how to hold a successful garage sale. Did you know there are books published now explaining how to stage a garage sale? You can sell your copy at your next sale.

I'll tell you a few funny ideas. One is from Amy Dacyczyn's *The Tightwad Gazette II*, in which she suggests "weaving" plastic six-pack rings into volleyball nets or hammocks. Oh my.

Another dates from my childhood. My mother used to give all our family's stuff to the nuns who did our laundry. They took my father's old, gigantic, exposed X-ray negatives, bleached them snow-white and turned them into notebook covers, wallets, and doll's booties, stitched together with bright yarn and decorated with enamel paint.

Oh, and during World War II we were shown how to reuse old 78 rpm records by soaking them in hot water until they were malleable and then molding them into bowls. Ugliest things you ever saw. And they leaked.

The Tightwad also suggests using a hot-glue gun and the plastic tabs from bread bags to repair plastic laundry baskets and other plastic items. (I would really like a time-cost analysis on how much money this saves against what your time is worth.) You can also use hot glue to repair sneakers, if they fit anyone you know. I use a pair of old sneakers when I wash my down coat and quilts in the commercial size washers at the Laundromat. They bounce around in the tub with the items and keep the filling from piling. If you do this, don't expect to wear the sneakers again because they shrink.

The second part of the Greater Vancouver Guide, the "Resource Directory," is just that – a big list of charities, clubs, organizations and stores, with a description of what they will buy, sell, repair, or rent.

Some of the activity that recyclers get into sounds pretty funny and is easily satirized. However, what is not funny is the fact that we have just about squeezed Earth dry and we, in North America, are the ones who are most to blame. I have some shocking figures, taken from an American source, The New Road Map Foundation, but bear with me.

- Though a mere 8 percent of all humans on this planet own cars, 89 percent of American households do.
- The amount of energy used by one American equals that used by
  - 3 Japanese
  - 6 Mexicans
  - 14 Chinese
  - 38 Indians
  - 531 Ethiopians and Eritreans.

- Since 1940, Americans have used up as large a share of Earth's mineral resources as all previous generations on Earth put together.

Canada is not far behind in these areas of consumption. In fact, I know from other sources that Canadians talk more on the telephone than any other people in the world, and Canadians use even more energy (fossil fuel). I attribute both of these extravagances to the cold climate.

This is one area where it would be good for all of us to suffer sharp, severe and unending pangs of guilt, so bad that we will be compelled by inner demons to mend our wasteful ways. We must develop total, bleeding-heart compassion for the poor and disadvantaged of the world and take responsibility for the part we have played in making them even worse off than they were and for widening the sickening gap between the haves and have-nots. This is not a simple problem, and not to be solved by simplistic, saving ways. Mere Band-Aids won't do much to stop the hemorrhaging. We can't reduce the complexity of Earth's problems to quick bytes and expect to solve them with simple solutions. T-shirt slogans, graffiti and bumper sticker aphorisms, while succinct and amusing, are also dangerous. Three or four Rs are only the beginning of a massive consciousness-raising that must take place in the minds and hearts of human beings. Try these (my list):

- Remind
- Reawaken
- Renew
- Restore
- Resurrect
- Revitalize.

Six Rs for the future of the planet! Not as simple as they sound.

Two-time Pulitzer Prize winner Edward O. Wilson, considered the dean of biodiversity studies in the world, is required reading for those who care about our planet's health. In spite of all we talk about it, he says, we're doing "a wretched job at protecting and managing the environment.

"In 1946, when I started college," he said, in an interview with *The Globe and Mail*, July 21, 1997, "there were two billion people on Earth. Now there are 5.7 billion; in 30 years there will be eight billion."

Wilson thinks we should pay attention to the fact that the have-nots of the world are multiplying at a greater rate than the haves. He pointed out that while in 1946, two-thirds of humanity lived in the developing countries, that figure has increased to four-fifths. In 30 years Third World people will comprise five-sixths of this planet. One billion of them – the bottom billion, they are called – struggle for survival from one day to the next, living in what the United Nations classifies as absolute poverty. A half-million children die each year from starvation or starvation-related diseases. These are human beings, fellow inhabitants of this planet.

As the poet W. H. Auden said, "We must love one another or die." Dead simple.

8

Community

A society can be judged by the way it treats
its most disadvantaged, its least beloved,
its mad. As things now stand,
we must be judged a poor lot, and it is time to mend our ways.
– Lewis Thomas

We're going to encounter the concept of community a lot as we proceed toward simplicity. I'm not talking about communal living; I mean community co-operation. It's going to come up in reference to housing, and of course to bartering, swapping, trading, and ultimately currency. That's community.

community n. pl. **-ties.**
1. a group of people having common ties or interests and living in the same locality or district and subject to the same laws: a farming community. *This lake provides water for six communities.*
2. a group of people living together: *a community of monks.*
3. the public: *the approval of the community.*
4. ownership together; sharing together: *community of food supplies, community of ideas.*

5. a group of animals and plants living in a particular region under similar conditions and interacting with one another, especially in food relationships.
6. likeness, similarity; identity: *Community of interests causes people to work together.*[1]

We think that our pioneer ancestors with their quilting bees and barn-raisings relied on each other for unpaid, reciprocal help more than we do now. Not so. Only the activity has changed. Now we have car pools and Block Parents and networking. Same idea. One thing hasn't changed; the casseroles and sandwiches, spare beds, messenger and pickup services freely offered at a time of crisis, like illness or an accident or death in the family. No need to legislate this or write rules about it. It just happens, arising out of sympathy and neighborliness. This is the kind of community support that lies at the very heart of simple living, the assurance that other human beings are there when you need them. People are more interactive than anybody. It's too easy to get maudlin about this. Rather than do so, I offer a bouquet of thoughts from other writers.

Remember Robert Frost's *The Death of the Hired Man*?

> *Home is the place where, when you have to go there,*
> *They have to take you in.*

Here's an idea I want to keep working on in my own life:[2]

> *When I give, I give myself.*
> – Walt Whitman

And this is one of the toughest orders in the Book:

> *Thou shalt love thy neighbor as thyself.*
> – Leviticus 19:18

While remembering this one keeps us all humble:

No man is an island, entire of itself;
every man is a piece of the continent,...
– John Donne

There are, of course, artificial communities that have sprung up around a set of often rigid rules for living, cult societies dedicated to simplicity but based on compulsion. These are not the kind of community we have in mind when we speak of the sharing and caring that goes on in a simple society. Still, we must share some of the characteristics of the bee, with a drive to hive. If people hadn't invented communities, God would have had to because most of us can't bear to be alone for long. In my research I have come across clubs, societies, groups, alliances, associations, and co-ops each with its handle on simplicity. I'll begin with a few familiar names. (For addresses and Web sites, see Appendix 1.)

I've already mentioned E. F. Schumacher (*Small is Beautiful*). The E. F. Schumacher Society was founded in 1980 in Great Barrington, MA, to promote the ideas in his book by presenting them in programs combining economics, ecology and culture. Since 1981 the society has conducted an Annual Lecture Series, and these lectures are available through its publication service. The Second Annual Decentralist Conference was held in June 1997, with the focus on people, land, and community. There is also a Schumacher Society in Great Britain. You'll meet Schumacher again when we come to SHARE (see p.184).

The World Stewardship Institute based in California seems to have a line on New Zealander Marilyn Waring, having sponsored a recent lecture: "Who's Counting? Marilyn Waring on Sex, Lies, and Global Economics." The institute, recognizing that "the health of the world economy is dependent on the health of the Earth and its biosphere," was established to promote "environmental leadership and innovation in business, science and religion."

Duane Elgin is the inspiration of the Simple Living Network with its own press which publishes *Simple Living: The Journal of Voluntary Simplicity*, a quarterly magazine devoted to – you guessed it – the promulgation of voluntary simplicity. There's an online newsletter, and a whole network of Support Groups and Study Circles (52 at last count and 11 in Canada) to be joined for the asking, or you can start your own.

The Phinney Neighborhood Association, another large spin-off, offers a Friday Forum Series with Voluntary Simplicity Classes and a compendium of resources. The idea may be aimed at developing a simpler lifestyle, but the pile of information and stuff collecting around it is getting very complicated indeed.

The Pierce Simplicity Study is not an association so much as it is an exploration of the simple living lifestyle trend. "What is this simplicity trend all about, anyway?" it asks on its home page. The organizers send out an impressive bibliography of books in the field and offer an even more exhaustive one in return for your time and energy in filling out a survey. When I have time, I will – that is, when I finish writing this book (maybe I can sell it to them). The Pierce analysis of the simplicity trend is one of the richest and most succinct of any I have come across, including the many attempts to explain what Duane Elgin is all about.

There is no doubt that the head gurus of this decade are Vicki Robin and the late Joe Dominguez. The New Road Map Foundation, which they established to siphon off the embarrassing amount of money they have made on their bestselling book *Your Money or Your Life*, is staffed by nine full-time volunteers who also don't need the money because they achieved their independence by following the nine-step program in the book. What an affidavit! What a community!

Bill Henderson heads a unique, quirky, practical club whose time has come. The Lead Pencil Club for confirmed Luddites – but they let scabs in, too – was founded in 1993, when Henderson says some Luddite sentiments he came across in Doris Grumbach's memoir *Extra Innings* triggered a response. She had complained about her word processor which set him to wondering. "Why not use a lead pencil?" That led to the thought, "Why not a Lead Pencil Club, for those of us who agree with her?"

When he found out that Henry David Thoreau was the son of a pencil maker and helped his dad make pencils, it seemed too serendipitous to ignore. Henderson likes to think that *Walden* was written with a pencil made by the good hermit himself, and named the writer the founder emeritus of the new club. Word of pencil, mouth, and eventually news services around the world, brought in a surprising response. Henderson welcomes all comers, no questions asked, though people seem eager to state their qualifications. No dues, either, but you can buy a T-shirt to help pay for a book[3] Henderson edited, with a blue pencil, no doubt. Occasionally he writes a newsletter on his 1942 Royal manual typewriter. There is simplicity as well as humor in this fellowship. The book, a collection of essays and comments from the members, pokes eloquent fun at many of the things in our lives today that the serious simpletons are trying to scuttle. As one writer puts it, downscaling and upshifting leads to around-the-bend-going.

Luddite has become a label computer-illiterates fasten on themselves these days with a kind of inverse pride which would baffle the instigator of it all. In about 1779, a feeble-minded Leicestershire village lad named Ned Ludd broke into a stockinger's one day and smashed the framing machines, such an act of vandalism that after that, whenever the stocking equipment in the hosiery district was damaged, people would say, "Ludd must have been here." He wasn't the last.

From 1811 to 1816, textile workers began breaking the machinery they blamed for their job losses. Inspired by their imaginary hero, General Ned Ludd, these self-styled Luddites staged riots and demonstrations all over England to protest the new technology that threatened their livelihood. The title and the attitude lives on in New Luddites who claim a 200-year tradition of campaigning against the legitimacy of science and any technology which they perceive as a threat to the planet. Although they are uncomfortable with E-mail (criticizing it as too exclusive and also threatening to postpersons), the present-day Ned Ludd has set up an address with Green-Net, part of the Association for Progressive Communications. New Luddites say of themselves that they are a dis-organization, meaning "no distant leadership, no formal membership, no AGMs and no subs." However, "any donations, contributions, artistic abuse, are very welcome" (see Appendix 1).

Not all of the people who claim they want to live "contraption-free" are as amused or amusing as Bill Henderson and his pencil-pushers. Some Luddites go so far as to acknowledge a relationship to the former math professor alleged to be the murderous Unabomber, or at least claim to understand his resentment of industrial society. Another Luddite, Kirkpatrick Sale, not quite so violent, limits his protests to smashing computers with a sledgehammer. He and poor feeble-minded Ned would get along just fine. Community is where you find it.

The whole idea of sustainability – and there are many definitions – appears to have its driving center on the West Coast where the Simple Living Network and the New Road Map Foundation originated. Sustainable Seattle, founded in 1991, is a long-term cultural, economic, environmental network run by volunteers who take to the streets with community outreach projects. Other West Coast organizations with similar goals include Context Institute (Bainbridge Island, WA); and the University of Washington Center for Sustainable Communities (Seattle), enabling research on the sustainability of communities in Seattle and Cascadia. (Cascadia has a Home Page of its own.)

The Worldwatch Institute, based in Washington, DC (for a change), is another organization dedicated to "fostering the evolution of an environmentally sustainable society, one in which human needs are met in ways that do not threaten the health of the natural environment or the prospects of future generations." Believing, as we all do, that information is a powerful tool of social change, the institute publishes a magazine. Well and good, but if you're trying to cut down, go easy on all the subscriptions.

I expected there to be a Walden Association but I can't find one. Though we all stand upon the shoulders of giants, very few people these days notice whose shoulders gave them the boost. I did come upon a Walden Home Page with a "Henry David Thoreau Campfire Chat" and a very unlikely URL (see Appendix 1).

One of the more bizarre organizations is The Media Foundation (TMF), an assembly of media activists intent on "counteracting those who would pollute our physical and mental environments." Claiming they are "neither left nor right, but straight ahead," they run Powershift Advocacy Agency

(PAA). PAA focuses the energies of these social marketers and media activists on 30-second spots and print ads that try to raise public awareness of the effects of the media. They have produced a TV Uncommercial, a 30-second, broadcast quality video which they will supply free of charge to anyone who can get it on a local community station (not too expensive during the day). They welcome other advocacy groups to join them. Check out their Web site and URL. They also publish *Adbusters* magazine.

The language of the magazine is known as *culture jamming* which can include political satire, humorous spoofs of commercial culture, sci-fi probes into cyberspace or scholarly ones into the decline of civilization. The most decadent aspect of civilization that TMF attacks each year is consumer spending. Buy Nothing Day (BND), with fronts around the world, was launched in 1992 in Canada by Ted Dave. It's now a global action day – or non-action, depending on how you look at it. Originally set on a nondescript date, this 24-hour moratorium on consumer spending has been staged for the last five years on the day after American Thanksgiving, long recognized in the United States as the biggest shopping day of the year, the go-signal for the Christmas blowout.

By 1996, BND was celebrated in ten countries around the world by non-shoppers who ran ads, hung posters, held rallies, cut up their credit cards and performed street theater. A 30-second spot, created in Canada by The Media Foundation, ran during the CNN Headline News: an animated pig demonstrated the excesses of consumerism. Some television networks (NBC, ABC, and CBS) refused to run the Uncommercial. When Rush Limbaugh saw it on CNN, he was shocked, which delighted the organizers.

In Montreal, the 1996 event was staged by the Concordia and McGill Quebec Public Interest Research Groups in the basement of St. James United Church, where people gathered to swap and exchange things rather than buy them, and listened to the Buy Nothing Day choir who performed alternative Christmas carols in two downtown shopping malls as well as the church basement. They tried to sing in the Montreal Eaton Centre but they were ejected. Poor Eaton's. I can understand why they wouldn't appreciate people warning people not to buy anything. In Seattle a group called the Raging Grannies sang in their local mall, and I understand the rage has traveled to grannies in the Toronto area. These ladies also distributed a press release and wound up on PBS.

Buy Nothing Day is anti-consumerism at its most virulent. For 1997, the Foundation broadcast in the capitals of all the G7-plus nations and placed a full-page ad in the *New York Times*, and instructed its members to dress up like CEOs, using pig snouts made from pink egg cartons (12 to a carton) and a little string. TMF provided (on loan) a free broadcast copy of the BND ad, and sold or gave instructions to make BND T-shirts. Concerned consumers were also encouraged to find their own ways to protest. Depending on your skills and enthusiasm/rage, you too can join in by dropping out of the rat race. Hang a BND poster, pass out pamphlets, write your own press release, sing an anti-shopping carol, cut up your credit cards, give "Christmas Gift Exemption Vouchers,"[4] but above all – *Don't Buy Anything!*

The latter is not as easy as it sounds. These days, even breathing costs money, depending on whether the air is cooled or heated, humidified or de-, or freshened with aromatic dispensers. I pay for my drinking water because my pure northern lake water is no longer fit for consumption. You will have to resist temptation with all your non-consuming power. Who knows? You may topple governments – or at least shopping malls.

There are other Canadian assemblies of interested communities, not the least of them the awesome LETSystems just now unleashing its power (see Community Currencies, p. 186). One of the most attractive groups with a recycling focus is the Greater Vancouver Regional District (GVRD). It offers an encyclopedic collection of ways to reuse and recycle (see p. 83) in a book with the intriguing title *101 Ways to Reuse Your Old Shoes 'N Other Stuff: A Money-Saving Guide to Reusing, Repairing, and Renting Goods in the Lower Mainland*. It also has a resource directory. GVRD's goal is to reduce by 50 percent the amount of garbage produced in the area by the year 2000. Judging by the book, I think they're going to have fun doing it.

As is typical of Canada, a number of our associations are rooted in academia. For example, the Faculty of Environmental Studies at the

University of Waterloo has been publishing a quarterly journal called *Alternatives*, a magazine about the environment, for 26 years. The Canadian Co-operative Association (CCA) has its fingers in so many pies the mind boggles. Together with the Centre of the Study of Co-operatives, it maintains a Web site with useful information about several aspects of co-operative community effort that are of interest to people wanting to simplify their lives. CCA, on the Web, provides information about and a link to the Association of Canadian Childcare Co-operatives, a recently formed national group concentrating on staff development, working with parents and maintaining co-op child care.

Similarly, Women in Co-operatives Electronic Network (WICEN) is an Internet-based forum open to anyone with a modem and E-mail address. I love the acronym; it reminds me of *wiccan* (the modern adjective, based on the Old English plural of *wicca*), the word used today to refer to the entire religion of witchcraft. I bet it was on purpose. WICEN, moderated by CCA, is designed to provide a forum for an exchange of ideas, to network and make new contacts, with the discussion aimed at women-related issues, among them, family-friendly policies and practices in co-ops, plus marketing to women.

CCA also offers instructions for starting a co-operative, with links to different provinces (British Columbia, Saskatchewan, Ontario, so far). Most co-operatives are regulated by provincial legislation so each province must have its own constitution. Co-ops, of course, are business organizations owned by the members who use their services, functioning examples of simplified living. If the co-op is created to provide work, the workers are the member-owners; if to purchase goods and services, the members are the consumers (buyers). Co-ops can be either for-profit or not-for-. In Canada, most co-ops in the healthcare, childcare and housing sectors are not-for-profit. Some co-ops may receive government funding (for example, family housing), but they are not government organizations. Co-ops are community based and initiated, and offer a means of controlling the economic, social and cultural activities affecting their members. The only co-ops I'm going to discuss are those to do with housing (see p.137).

Canadians – Concern about Violence in Entertainment (C-CAVE) is not quite a spin-off but a corollary of The Cultural Environment Movement (CEM), both deeply concerned about the effects of television violence on children. George Gerbner, the founder of CEM, says there is no such thing as "happy violence."

Taking a positive approach to the media is the Canadian Association for Media Education British Columbia (CAME), established in 1991. Working in co-operation with the British Columbia Teachers' Federation (BCTF), CAME has a triple mandate:

- to educate Canadians about the media
- to promote media education
- to encourage Canadian cultural expression in the media.

So far the association has produced a TV and news curriculum, a conceptual framework for media education, two resource samplers, and it supplies speakers on request, with variable fees.

The Social Investment Organization (SIO) is another Canadian group which deals with ethical investing (see p. 123). They also participate in the Socially Responsible Business (SRB) Discussion Group, a free online look at ethical investment and business issues, used mainly by US researchers but Canadian subscribers log on as well.

I could go on and on. You may infer that these examples I have cited are a mere sample of the kind of interactive, globally concerned, ecologically conscientious communites all related in one way or another to our concerns. A simple sampling?

"Community of interests," according to the last definition from the *Gage Canadian Dictionary*, "causes people to work together." In a way it's the exact opposite of Zen. Instead of listening to the sound of one hand clapping, we admire the way two hands wash each other. Co-ops can exist on any scale for any purpose, but the mutual hand-washing image is a good one to keep in mind. The co-op movement, comments Saskatchewan writer E. Forrest Scharf, "makes for altruism as against selfishness; it gives people self-respect when they find that they are, after all, able to do something in the way of managing their own social and economic affairs, when the truth comes home to them that business ability is not something to be found in only a few human beings, but that there is a certain amount of it in everybody. From this experience they acquire confidence in themselves, develop an awareness of their duties and obligations to themselves and to other members of the human race."[5]

Aldo Leopold was the author of a beautiful nature book called *A Sand County Almanac*, a modern-day *Walden* if there ever was one. Leopold died in 1948 when the book was in draft form, but his son Luna edited it, along with other unpublished essays and journals which became a second book called *Round River*. The two books were combined in a new edition (1966) and offer dazzling descriptions of the wildlife and natural resources of this continent along with a searing criticism of what's happening to them in the name of progress and financial rewards. "That land is a community," Leopold wrote in 1948, "is the basic concept of ecology, but that land is to be loved and respected is an extension of ethics."

We are members of a larger co-operative than most of us bother to recognize. If human beings don't co-operate in the protection of our home and the source of all our livelihood, there won't be one. We must not forget this largest community – Earth. We think we don't owe her any dues, but the fines are horrendous when we break her rules. Drain the marshes to plant wheat and watch where the water goes when the rivers spill. Clear away all the trees and watch the dust bowls drink up life. We must co-operate; we must bear the responsibility and pay our dues.

PART IV

Making Dollars Make Sense

It's about identifying, for yourself, what you need as opposed to what you want, what purchases or types of purchases actually bring you fulfilment, what represents "enough" to you and what you actually spend money on.

– Joe Dominguez and Vicki Robin

9

Budgeting

Having great wealth is one of the most disappointing things.
It's overrated, I can tell you that. It's not as good as average sex.
Average sex is better than being a billionaire.
– Ted Turner[1]

Most of us will never become one of the 358 billionaires of the world, but most of us can manage average sex. I hope that comforts you as I set about telling you how to live with the money you have, or less. Since this is primarily a philosophical book rather than a money manual, I think it is also appropriate here to refer you to a story by Leo Tolstoy that I read in school a hundred years ago, so I don't know if it's still on the curriculum. How many of you are familiar with the story, "How Much Land Does a Man Need?"

A man starts walking at the crack of dawn to measure out a parcel of land. He will be granted as much as he can cover on foot in a day, returning to the starting point at sundown. His eyes are bigger than his legs. He keeps pushing himself just a little farther and a little farther until, when he finally turns back late in the day, realizing how far he has come and how far he has to go to get back, he pushes harder, racing with pumping lungs and heart to return to the finish line. He reaches it just as the sun goes down, and dies. He needs six feet of land to be buried in. Tolstoy never was a jolly writer.

Still, it's a good parable to carry with you when you're tempted to bite off more than you can chew, or to take on more debt than you can comfortably carry (debt is never comfortable!), or to strive for something you'll never achieve and if you do you won't enjoy it anyway, you'll want more or something else. We are mistaken when we quote Browning[2] who said, "Ah, but a man's reach must exceed his grasp/Or what's a heaven for?" He was talking about artistic creation which is quite different, or is it? Aspiring artists stub their toes and bark their knees and bash their heads against the gates of creation, though few are allowed to enter. (I know.) Browning's heaven is the goal, the ideal standard of perfection to which all artists must aspire. At the moment, you're no artist and you're not looking for perfection. You're looking for less stress and more satisfaction, simplicity without pain. If that's not it, exactly, then figure out what you do want. Whatever it is, you know that you'll need a certain amount of money to make it happen. Even the simplest of lifestyles costs a certain amount to maintain. Man cannot live by bread alone, nor woman neither, but no one can live without bread. Unless you are a genuine lily of the field, you're going to need money to live.

Jacob Needleman, in his book *Money and the Meaning of Life*, tries to persuade his readers to learn more about money and to adopt a different attitude to it, claiming that we don't take money seriously enough, that we have come to know the price of everything and the value of nothing. (I've heard that line before. It sounds Wilde to me.[3]) He thinks we have to pay close attention to the way we handle sex, time, and money, these three, because no one has given "serious and useful thought [to] the relationship between the quest for money and the quest for meaning. The fact is, whatever your dreams, no matter how simple, they're going to cost money to realize.

"It is very good to say that one should be poorer," Needleman continues, "but money seems to help." Especially if you don't have it. Whether you're rich or whether you're poor, it's always nice to have money. So let's pause and figure out how to have it, or at least what to do with whatever we have.

Budget

Before you begin to tailor a realistic budget for yourself, you have to know how much you spend – oh, and how much you take in, that would help. First, though, figure out where the money goes.

Don't buy a new notebook. You must have an old scribbler around the house, maybe even a notepad with graphed lines that you bought some time in a fit of good intention to keep track of where the money goes. Do it now. Keep track of where the money goes. For three months.

Other advisers will tell you to keep watch for only a month. Not enough. In our money book,[4] Lynne Macfarlane and I say three months. That way you won't cheat. You might skip something you normally spend money on if it's only for a month. To look good on paper, you can do without it, for a month. Unless you've made a new year's resolution that you are never going to eat another chocolate-covered nutball in your entire life, you will – buy it and eat it – in the second month. And you think you can easily skip the magazine you usually pick up at the newsstand but the third month there's an article you can't resist or a centerfold you have to have and before you know it, you've forked out $4.75 plus tax, and that's where the money goes. So be aware.

When you have this record of your secret life, sit down and take a good hard look at it and yourself (and your family). You'll find that the first step toward saving money is like heating your house: you have to plug the leaks to stop the warmth/money from running out the holes. Most people are dismayed, maybe even shocked and appalled, at the amount of money they let dribble through their fingers. Most people actually lose weight when they stop dribbling. You'll be amazed how much cash you spend on things like chocolate bars and soda pop and carrot bran muffins with your coffee and hash brown laminates with your Egg Mcwhatsits. You'll probably quit or cut back. You just started a budget.

You don't do that, you say. You have a very firm grip on yourself and your wallet. Okay. Try this: take with you each day exactly the amount of money you need for parking, transit, coffee, whatever. Put a hundred dollar bill in a secret compartment in case you're in an accident or find exactly the mother-of-pearl inkwell you've been looking for all your life. Most people won't break a hundred without a very good reason; chances are you'll carry it until it's threadbare on the folds. Did I mention you should leave your credit card(s) at home as well? Unless you have to gas up the car. Now tell me you didn't dribble your money away because I'm telling you that a very good way not to spend money is not to carry it. Poor people have no trouble understanding this. Oh – maybe you should allow some "spare," as they call it, change for the street beggars. Better yet, write a monthly check to the fresh produce branch of a food bank, feed someone (children, I hope) some decent food, and get a tax credit while you're at it.

Credit cards will take away even more of your money, they're so painless. They don't feel like spending. I've seen estimates that a person's spending increases anywhere from 10 to 25 percent when using a credit card. Impulses as well as debts soar. I lost my wallet once just before Christmas. I knew it was lost, not stolen, so I didn't report anything. (One of my kids found it for me, eventually.) I just ran on cash and stopped when I ran out. January of that year I had no debts. You'd think I might have learned something, but I didn't. I did, however, cancel all my credit cards but one, and I always pay the full amount owing each month. I let the company do my bookkeeping for me. I'm still talking budget, just trying to plug some serious holes before we get serious about the whole security blanket.

Now, apart from the dribbles, figure out where your big money is going, on an annual basis. This way, you'll know at a glance what you need to live for a year. I call it my nut. Later, when you tot up your monthly expenses, you can divide by 12 and add in the monthly amount. You may not want to do this; I have to because I don't have a regular salary. I have to think in lump sums. So I start with fixed expenses, not forgetting income tax which, if you're self-employed, may be hard to calculate but is here to stay. You may feel more comfortable going to the detailed form beginning on page 106.

Annual Expenses

Expense	Amount
House payments (mortgage, rent)	_____
House taxes	_____
Life/disability insurance	_____
House & contents insurance	_____
Car insurance	_____

I add:

Utilities (gas, electricity, etc.)[5] _____

I also have now added:

Car lease payments _____

And you'd better give a thought to:

Transportation costs (gas, oil, license) _____

You might like to add:

Christmas/gifts _____

And some people like to plan on:

Travel _____

And here is a must:

Food (!) _____

And another imperative:

Savings (10 percent of your annual income) _____

RRSP[6] _____

And please include:

Charitable donations[7] _____

TOTAL _____

There now. Once you see your total yearly expenditure, it's easier to break it down into 12 monthly portions, and make sure it's there. Then you know how much money you need to have each month to cover the crisis. I say the crisis because there's always a crisis – every month. I discovered that when I was first widowed and coping with money for the first time in my life. I lurched from crisis to crisis. What I wanted desperately was a no-surprises budget. Mind you, I find it a little more difficult than most people because the next thing most of you have to do is align your outgo with your income, which, if you have a regular job, you already know. I do not have a regular job, therefore, have no regular income. So when I look at my projected nut, the next thing I have to do is figure out whether I'll make enough money to cover it. I project my probable income and see how far I will fall short. I usually have to plan on another assignment or two before I can begin to balance my budget.

Anyway, now that you know yourself so well – what you need and what you spend – you should be able to fill in the blanks on the next set of columns fairly easily. This is designed for you to refer back to regularly. It's another way of keeping track and taking steps to plug the leak before it's too late. Here you go:

Monthly Budget

ITEM	PLANNED	ACTUAL
Income	_____	_____
Outgo		
Annual Expenses (total divided by 12)		
Savings (*Pay yourself first!*)	_____	_____
Property Taxes	_____	_____
Insurance		
house	_____	_____
car	_____	_____
life and/or disability	_____	_____

Gifts (including Christmas)   _____   _____

Travel   _____   _____

RRSP   _____

Housing[8]

  mortgage/rent payments   _____   _____

  electricity   _____   _____

  gas (heating, cooking)   _____   _____

  water   _____   _____

  telephone   _____   _____

  maintenance (repairs)   _____   _____

  supplies   _____   _____

Transportation[9]

  car (purchase, lease, share)[10]   _____   _____

  gas, oil, washes   _____   _____

  repairs   _____   _____

  parking   _____   _____

  licence   _____   _____

  taxis (travel?)   _____   _____

  public transit   _____   _____

Food

  groceries   _____   _____

  eating out[11]   _____   _____

  booze[12]   _____

Personal

  health care/insurance[13]   _____   _____

  prescriptions   _____   _____

  dental care

  hair   _____   _____

Clothes   _____   _____

Help[14]

  clones   _____   _____

  elves   _____

  fairy godmothers   _____   _____

Necessary Stimuli (not drugs)

entertainment	_____	_____
books/magazines/newspapers[15]	_____	_____
cable television/videos	_____	_____
continuing education (?)	_____	_____
health club/exercise/green fees...	_____	_____
hobbies (craft materials;	_____	_____
camera/camcorder/film;		
jigsaw puzzles....)		

Miscellaneous

This is where you put in all that stuff		
you've been cheating on: chocolate		
bars and gum (food??); a duck basket	_____	_____

TOTAL EXPENSES	_____	_____
BALANCE (over/under plan)	_____	_____

Now all you have to do is total your expenses and subtract this number from the number on the very top line, your income. If the result is a positive number, you will sleep well tonight because you're bringing in more than you're doling out. If the result is a negative number – that is, minus – you will see how serious you have to get with your money and your life. Your aim is to bring your ends together, so that they meet. Everyone should make ends meet, or what's a heaven for?

I've already confessed that I am a bookaholic and I really am trying to behave. Several years ago I managed to stop buying so many cookbooks when I realized that if I started to try all the recipes I own every day for the rest of my life, I would never get through them all. I tell myself the same about my books. It will take me a lifetime to read all the books I already own, and yet I keep buying more. I'm sure other bibliophiles will admit that the very purchase of a book is almost the same as reading it. I keep thinking there is one more thing I need to learn and then I will have the whole secret of life. In my saner moments, I realize it's in me and not in a book. What am I saying? Of course, you are going to learn the secret of simple living. You may never have to buy another book, not like this one, at any rate from me.

And also at any rate, you're making progress if you face the fact that you will be making frugality a way of life. However, before that happens, you can effect a few changes in your basic approach. Pardon me if I'm simplistic about this, but this is what this book is. Here are a few simple rules.

- Don't spend money you haven't got.
- The easiest way to save money is not to spend it.
- Don't spend money on new expenses.
- Don't spend money on new, increased fixed expenses.[16]
- Don't sign on for book clubs, either.
- Don't spend money when you can save by doing something else, or making do.
- Don't spend money on meat – or spend less.
- Don't spend money on food you can prepare yourself.
- Don't spend money on telephone calls at expensive times.
- Don't spend money when you can spend time – on people, gifts, calls, service for yourself and others.
- Don't spend money on anything that costs over $10 without thinking twice and making sure you need it.

The Canadian jurist and author T. C. Haliburton, best remembered for *The Clockmaker* (1836), an account of the sayings and doings of a sharp Yankee peddler named Sam Slick, made an astute comment about what we're discussing. "It is easier," he wrote, "to make money than to save it; one is expertise, the other is self-denial." Astute, but not entirely true these days. Making money can be very stressful, making more money even more so. The trick is to look for ways to cut expenses without feeling denied. You aren't even going to feel the loss of some of those dribbles.

But if you must make more money, and a lot of people do these days, just to make ends meet because someone keeps moving the ends, then consider a few ploys. Some of them are one-shot; you may never come this way again. Others might be useful to fall back on in a pinch.

I was in Russia very shortly after it ceased to be the USSR, when people were beginning to feel squeezed by a so-called capitalist society with no capital, and trying to cope. There was a path parallel to a river across from our hotel and it was lined every afternoon with people selling their household goods: icons and family heirlooms, handmade lace, wrought-iron pokers and andirons, shell-edged picture frames – genuine, touching treasures along with any schlock they could pick up that might get them a buck – an American buck. I've already told you about selling off my grandmother's letters and programs, as well as my back issues of magazines. You can do that.

A few years ago, after I moved in here, I had a new kitchen built: some decent shelves to replace the plywood cottage special you find in most cottages. When I began to put things back in the cupboards, even after I had rid myself of so much when I moved here, I found more stuff to get rid of. Too remote for a yard sale, no garage for a garage sale, I paid a fee to the local Lionnesses Club for a table in their annual Flea Market Sale, and persuaded a friend to come and help me move and sell stuff there – a very good friend because she bought some of my stuff herself! I sold her the guitar I meant to but never did learn how to play, and threw in all the sheet music; and a used electronic keyboard I was going to write songs on but never did. On my consumers at large I foisted my old stove (I had bought a new one for the new space), a redundant but functioning toaster, well polished; a set of brass fireplace tools, ditto, that I never used; on and on, you get the idea. I made $325 after expenses (my rental fee). You could do that.

You could also sell your services as a clone (see clone, p. 235). Once when I was doing a reading tour in Alberta and was short of money, I planned and cooked the meals for a friend of mine and her husband, for two weeks, in return for room and board, and left her with a freezer full of muffins. On more than one occasion I baby-sat the basset hounds for my friends in Bermuda in return for a place to write while they went away, secure in the knowledge that I wouldn't eat all the chococate chip cookies my friend had stashed in her freezer for her children's next visit as the previous house-sitter had done. I looked after plants in New York while their owners went on a trip, buying my own food but getting a fabulous apartment in the East 80s to play house in for two weeks. At my lowest ebb as a writer, I corrected the grammar in some Lottario brochures, a glorified typing job, and narrowly escaped doing some proofreading for another government department when I landed a good new assignment. You could do something like that. Moonlighting, as I have said elsewhere, becomes you, becomes any of us when we need a little extra money.

The best way, of course, to supplement your income, is with investments. Much easier on the nerves. So let us move on and talk about investing for less stress.

10

____

Investments for Income and Conscience

$100 placed at 7% interest compounded quarterly for 200 years will increase to more than $100,000,000 by which time it will be worth nothing.

– Lani's Principles of Economics,
from *The Official Rules*, Paul Dickson

There was an heiress at the turn of the century who was left with a sizeable sum in trust, so safely invested that she would never want for anything. Her advisers, spurning fly-by-night ventures, placed the young woman's entire fortune in a solid company whose product would always be in demand: stove blacking. As long as stoves needed cleaning, thought these dear, stolid trustees, their charge's money would be safe. Every home needed a wood-burning stove, and every housewife would keep hers polished. The moral to the story is that there is no such thing as a perfectly safe stock. Someone might invent electric stoves.

On the other hand, my husband's aunt, who went into business in a bank just after the end of World War I when she was 19, and who worked her way up over the next 46 years until, at her retirement, she was secretary to the provincial branch manager, took advantage of every good stock offer she came upon. Notably, she bought British American Oil in the 1930s, which split, and became Gulf Oil, then Gulf Western, and split and split again and kept on growing as she let her dividends accrue and compound until she had a very tidy sum to retire with. I interviewed another woman who bought Bell Telephone and Canadian Pacific at a very early age, with her first paychecks, and who never let them go – another rich old lady. Patience, I suppose, is a virtual bonanza when it comes to blue-chip. Now, what about you? You should live so long.

In the 1930s during the Depression that ended only with World War II, very few people invested. Investments were for rich people to hang themselves over when they failed. Ordinary people bought books on economics and played Monopoly and tried to understand what was going on, but they didn't invest. Conservative theory held that investments were like antiques: you didn't buy them until you had everything you needed, your house paid for, your children set for life, and your wife looked after. (Of course, all this advice was for men only.) Then you could play, if you felt like it. Dabble was the word. What happened? Investments hit the middle class shortly before the middle class began to shrink. Far from being a rich man's sport or a dilettante's toy, investments became a lifeline to the future, something like lottery tickets, something that could spring the lock on the mundane, money-grubbing trap of existence.

People who had never done so before began to play the stock market, looking for fast turnover and quick bucks. People who had always considered financial planners to be only for the very rich, were consulting theirs for the right moves to make. And then, just as they got impatient or burned or tired or scared, they discovered mutual funds.

Not that they hadn't existed, but the mind-set wasn't there. The first mutual fund, not called a mutual fund, was offered by a so-called open-end investment company, the Massachusetts Investors Trust, founded in 1924.[1] By the time of the crash (1929) the seemingly reluctant public had dumped more than $7 billion into investment companies. Then everyone fell off the cliff, but those who had money in unleveraged funds bounced a little more softly. The first Canadian mutual fund was Corporate Investors Limited, founded in 1931; the second was the Canadian Investment Fund, launched in 1932; the third, the Commonwealth International Corporation fund, started in 1933 – all three in the heart of the Depression when people could scarcely spare a dime. By 1949 the total assets of those first three funds totaled less than $20 million. After a 17-year gap, in 1950, Investors Mutual of Canada launched its first mutual fund and has been adding them ever since.[2] It's an idea whose time has come.

Mutual funds are like foot-warmers: comforting to have on a cold, bleak night when you are at your wit's end. You suffer from despair that you are ever going to get ahead, and cold feet because you're too scared to dip your icy toe in the swiftly moving current of the stock market. A mutual fund, as you already know, is a dispersed investment, dispersed because your guru (read: mutual fund manager) pools your mite with others' and invests the accumulated lump, thus giving you the benefit of his/her expertise, spreading your risk, saving you time and angst, and ultimately giving you a tidy, though not staggering, return on your money. If private investment clubs are what I call wading pools for timid investors, then mutual funds are indoor swimming pools, ideal for those who are not ready for the shark-infested rip tides of the ocean. Nothing is simple, of course.

Mutual funds have grown and increased ever since they hit the consciousness of an eager, nervous clientele until their numbers are beyond counting because their parents – the investment groups, trust companies, insurance companies, credit unions and banks – keep inventing new ones. There are money-market funds, the most liquid but the least profitable in times of low-interest (still a little better than the banks'), dependent for income on the interest from short-term paper like government treasury bills, with a customary time limit of no longer than 90 days. Equity funds are the most popular and come in lots of nationalities now (with a permitted limit of 20 percent foreign investment). These are best for long-term holding and offer the most reassuring promise of a good night's sleep. If, when all about you, stock markets are crashing and frantic investors are doing their high-wire act without a safety net, you may be serene with equity funds. Or so the story goes. You will remain serene as long as you don't need the money in a hurry. Be patient. Have trust. (That must be why a lot of financial institutions put trust in their titles.)

There are also fixed-income funds (bond funds – government, corporate and foreign – mortgage and mortgage bond funds), considered to offer a better return than your basic Guaranteed Investment Certificates (GICs) or savings accounts. You can be comfortable hanging on to these for three to five years.

Balanced funds are funds within funds, combinations of stocks and bonds whose dividends and interest, respectively, plus the prospect of capital gains, give people a sense of security for at least five years. You are usually well advised to allow the dividends to be automatically reinvested on a dollar cost averaging basis which allows you to keep on growing painlessly. Of course, you may prefer to receive and live on the dividends and or interest. That's the idea that Dominguez and Robin have in mind: with enough capital invested you can live – frugally or not, depending on the income you make – on the returns. Safety is all!

Funds keep on proliferating and diversifying: recent entries have been asset allocation funds and small cap funds, both of which have proved extremely popular with investors. The components of all these funds, the recipients of your hopes and money, that is, the companies and businesses and countries and governments you are investing in by proxy, are mixed and balanced and juggled by the wizards who handle them. Specialty funds abound: real estate, gold, resources, medical and high-tech funds. I often wonder how the wizards sleep.

Mutual funds are not only safe, they're also affordable. With a low down payment (initial investment) and a low monthly contribution after that, which varies with companies, you're off and running toward the no-load pot of gold at the end of the rainbow. Suddenly everyone believes in leprechauns (or financial wizards) but even these magic creatures can make mistakes. I'm sure you've seen the headlines when a major financial institution goes bust. It is possible to lose your life's savings so you do have to pay attention.

I'm sure the amount of money sitting in mutual funds today is equivalent to the combined budgets of most of the Third World countries with a couple of small European ones thrown in – billions and billions of dollars. Who owns all that wealth? We do, in fact – we, the investors. So why are we crying wolf, talking poor, and fretting about the future? Two reasons: One, we feel pressured. If we're so rich, why aren't we more relaxed? Two, we're all going to live so long we're afraid we'll last longer than our money. Good point.

In the meantime, what's so great about the rat race we're running? We're getting tired of it and the prize isn't that great, just another, bigger rat race. Thorstein Veblen had an impressive phrase for this materialistic competition we seem to find ourselves in: *pecuniary emulation*. More peculiar than pecuniary. Whom, after all, are we trying to emulate? The Joneses? They took early retirement already.

Is it, in fact, possible to live tomorrow today? Can we take our rewards before we die or retire, whichever comes first? Could someone show us, not how to live on what we earn – anyone can do that (well, we're trying) – but how to live on what we invest, so that maybe we won't have to work, as such. The answer is a resounding maybe.

Dominguez and Robin, authors of *Your Money or Your Life*, have led a lot of people to the promised land of dividends through a wise investment strategy and an even wiser approach to personal spending. It's called discretion, and it's quite simple: don't spend everything you bring in and invest the difference. The golden gurus say you have to find the "crossover point," the point at which your monthly investment income matches your monthly expenses. This is also called financial independence, a consummation devoutly to be wished. After that, you're laughing, working for yourself, for the sheer joy of it, not for need but for others. (Most of us are already working for others – our families.) When you have enough, say Dominguez and Robin, "you can consume or you can create." That's when you start making dreams come true, yours and others'. It sounds like a dream. I recommend you read the book for the details.

Now read it again and see if you think you can do it. The catch is that most people simply don't make enough money from other sources (that is, without working for pay) to be able to buy their freedom. I'm not saying it's hopeless. I'm not saying you have to get back in your cage and stay there until you die. I do think you can redefine the walls of your cell and maybe get some time out. I offer a more philosophical approach to the problem of when enough is enough.

Through the 1980s and just a squeak into the 1990s, perhaps, it was still possible to live a discreet, meager existence on the returns from safe, safe, safe, also secure, blue-chip investments. (That's why I told you those stories I began with.) It gets harder and harder as the market has been taking roller-coaster rides that put Canada's Wonderland to shame. At the time of writing, with interest rates so low the stock market outperforms the blue-chips any day, and don't even ask about GICs (Guaranteed Investment Certificates) and TDs (Term Deposits), it's difficult to know where to turn for returns. If you were to pay strict attention and could stand the stress of the market, you might make enough money to retire, or at least partly to withdraw from the aforementioned race. Maybe denial is a better route to peace of mind, in spite of what Thomas Haliburton's Sam Slick said about expertise. Denial and patience. And also don't be greedy. You can live with lower interest rates; you just need more capital. Time was, anyway, not so long ago, when usury was a sin.

Maybe the safest bet is to invest in your own country – for Canadians, that means Canada Savings Bonds (CSBs). Take the lower interest rates and stand on guard. Not to ignore provincial bonds or Canadian utilities – all reasonably safe. My friend Christopher Cottier has a quotable piece of advice: "Don't invest in anything younger than your children." As usual, with any pithy piece of advice, there is more to this than meets the eye. It means that as your children get older, so do you, and you shouldn't be taking flyers at your age. Play it a little safer as you and your children grow up. On the other hand, if you had invested in Bill Gates when he was 12, where would you be now?

We're not just talking about safe, liquid resources with steady returns and a long shelf life, though all of that is admirable. We're talking about conscience and consciousness, personal choice, values, and empowerment. Don't stop talking to your financial planner. If nothing else, it'll make her feel good. She likely won't remind you what Dominguez and Robin teach:

to sink your money into the safest, surest, steadiest, rock-hard investments you can find. Remember, you are not in this to make a killing. You want to make a living. Without working. Lots of luck.

Luck is a shaky foundation on which to base the rest of your life, so it's not a bad idea to hedge your bet and cushion your landing (and block that metaphor) with RRSPs. (I use the plural because you can have more than one RRSP.) This is not an exhaustive book of financial planning; I offer basic information so that you can choose what you want to investigate further on your own. By this time, even the financially challenged are aware that a Registered Retirement Savings Plan is supposed to be everyone's lifesaver in the future choppy seas of retirement or unemployment, whichever comes first. The federal government allows you to invest x percent (the amount depending on the whim of the feds) of your earned income annually in an investment shelter. The amount you put in and the amount you earn on interest or dividends within the plan is tax free until you cash it in at age 69 and take the entire sum of money thus accumulated (bad idea because it's taxable) or roll it into an annuity or a Registered Retirement Income Fund.

An RRIF is roughly the same as an RRSP in that it can hold all the investments you held in your RRSP, tax-sheltered, but there is a mandatory minimum withdrawal, increasing with your and its age until you hit (bump into) age 94 at which time the withdrawal rate is 20 percent of the total remaining in the fund. (You can base your minimum withdrawal on the age of a younger spouse, if you have one.). If you can live on the minimum, fine, but if you need new teeth or new wiring, you can withdraw a larger (taxable) amount. You decide how much you want or need in any given year (over and above the mandatory minimum annual withdrawal) and are thus provided with an income for life after work – you hope. Annuities also provide you with income but are less flexible than RRIFs, although there are variations on their theme. Right now RRIFs look better than annuities but if interest rates ever go up you may change your mind and convert all or part of your RRIF (only one per customer) to an annuity. You can shop around; you're good at that.

Like RRSPs, RRIFs and annuities are available through banks, mutual fund and trust companies, investment and brokerage houses, and credit unions. Although you must cash in your RRSP by the end of the year in which you turn 69, you can, if you want, do it sooner.[3] I've known people who wanted to launch a second trajectory career who cashed in their RRSPs at a much earlier age in order to go back to school for further education or training in a new skill. In that case, the tax bite is not too deep because income from other sources has been cut off. So it would be possible for you to downsize by taking what is popularly called early retirement and living on the proceeds of a well-planned RRIF or annuity. The key phrase is well-planned. To bring it off you have to start early, like with your first earned money – well, not with a paper route, unless you're 18 years old. But the trick is "to save early and save often," one of the popular aphorisms financial planners like to bandy about. (They also love to talk about the joys of compound interest.) Although the most popular advice is to save 10 percent of your income, if you're really intent on dropping out sooner, and staying out, then you'd better make that 20 percent (20 percent of after-tax income; let's be realistic here), and invest it wisely. If you do this, you won't need to cash in your RRSP(s) before it's time. Consider it an emergency fund. If you save and plan ahead this carefully you'll have simplified your life so much that by the time you take that first step into freedom it won't be any hardship to go on as you did with your frugal habits. That way your personal well won't run dry. May God grant you your health and your marbles and let's hope the money doesn't run out before you do.

Even when you want to simplify, it isn't simple. Not only do you have to plan on a steady supply of money from your investments, these days you have to worry about where that money is coming from.

Ethical Investments

Ethical investments started in the 1920s when the Methodist Church in North America began to invest in the stock market but wanted to avoid any companies involved in alcohol or gambling. The Quakers followed the Methodists and added weapons to their list of taboos. Once mutual funds with all their myriad interests were launched, could ethical mutual funds be far behind? They began in Vancouver in the early 1980s when Vancity Banks started Ethical Funds based on seven principles that are still roughly the same as the guidelines for screening the 15 mutual funds now operating in Canada. These criteria include progressive industrial relations; co-operative dealings (and respect) between staff and employees; the honoring of racial equality and equal opportunities; no military arms; no nuclear power; no tobacco/liquor; and observance of environmental concerns and regulations.

Ethical funds are known as feel-good investments because they make investors feel good about where their money is going and what it's doing for people and the planet. There are actually two kinds of such socially responsible investing.

1. Ethical investing is socially screened investing. You put your money in mutual funds, stocks, bonds or other securities that have been screened for you, assuring you that they represent ethical, environmental, social, political or moral values.

   For example, we (this is the corporate we) didn't invest in South Africa, as long as apartheid was going on (no one did!); we avoid arms and tobacco stocks. We're not too keen on nuclear power and weapons. Depends how strait-laced we are, whether we invest in whiskey or wine companies. We don't invest in countries with cruel dictatorships because we're concerned about human rights, however, we're not quite as smart at spotting sweatshops and often find ourselves (inadvertently?) investing in companies that mistreat and underpay their employees. We do not consider gold and jewelry to be ethical investments, and some people have an abhorrence of the nasty use of animals (trapping, testing).

2. Alternative investing is investment in companies or businesses with a community vision. Investors put their money in co-operative or community-oriented enterprises such as co-operatively-owned financial institutions, regional development bonds, not-for-profit enterprises or community loan funds. People who make these kinds of investments are helping to create local jobs and develop local enterprise (see SHARE as a good example, p. 184).

Financial experts maintain that ethical investments can peform as well as conventional investments that haven't been screened for their social values. It has been my observation that they are often cyclical in their returns and often in direct contrast to the performance of the hot stock of the month. That is, if companies whose products are verboten are in the ascendancy, ethical funds do not do well; on the other hand, if finances or electronic equipment are up, so are ethical funds. I don't know why that is. (If I did, I'd be rich.) Canada has 15 ethical mutual funds, in five different companies: The Clean Environment Fund, Desjardins Environmental, Dynamic Global Millenia, Ethical Funds, and Investors Summa Fund. They're all quite respectable in their performance and yields.[4]

Ethical investors like to think that they can change the world with their principles and principal. Not really, but by setting an example they might influence others, and by working with groups, in the case of co-op ventures, they help to bring their concerns to other people's attention. There are a lot of things out there to be concerned about. If some socially responsible investing helps you to another good night's sleep, then go for it.

The newest wrinkle in socially responsible investing in Canada is found in the Citizen's Bank, up and running on a Web site near you. With a home base in Vancouver, it's a virtual bank – no branches – providing services to customers by computer and phone. Eventually, says the blurb, every customer will be able to use the Internet, once it's safe from larcenous hackers (see encryption, p. 187). My bank is right in there or up there or out there with its virtual reality and pretend money – that is, money I never get to touch. I received a software package which I installed and now I can do most of my banking by computer.[5] I point this out to show how a non-bank works.

Where does social responsibility come in? The Citizen's Bank is the bank that underwrites LETSystems in Canada, a system of community currency designed to aid the economic development of the community and especially of people short of cash (see Community Currencies, p. 179).

The major source of information on ethical investing in Canada is the Social Investment Organization (SIO), a nationwide, nonprofit network of investors, business leaders and interest groups who believe that "corporate social responsibility and business success go hand in hand" – if not hand to mouth. They hold conferences and publish information covering social investment and corporate social performance issues such as workforce diversity, employee relations, the environment, corporate citizenship, community economics and international investment. The SIO also conducts research, analyzing the social and enironmental impact of Canadian industrial activity (see Appendix 1).

There are other sources of information about ethical investment. You might want to take a look at Chapter 8 in *The 1997 Canadian Ethical Money Guide* (updated annually) by Eugene Ellmen. The current volume provides new ratings of the 15 Canadian mutual funds and recommendations of major Canadian labor-sponsored investment funds.

It must be admitted that some so-called ethical investments are not terribly good ethics. You could end up in hours of debate discussing the finer points, and some people do. The Social Affairs Unit (SAU) is an independent research and educational trust with over 200 author-members devoted to the promotion of debate on social affairs and funded by a broad spectrum of foundations and trusts, with some 100 different sources. In 1996 author Dr. Digby Anderson, Director of SAU, engaged in a study in which he and some of his colleagues expressed their personal opinions about ethical investments, a discussion which was published. The commentators included Peter E. Hodgson, a Senior Research Fellow of Corpus Christi College, Oxford, and Head of the Nuclear Physics Theoretical Group of the Nuclear Physics Laboratory; writer and philospher Roger Scruton, formerly a professor at Boston University; and Professor Anthony O'Hear, Professor of Philosophy at the University of Bradford.

Their discussion revolved around the ambivalent attitudes to certain products. Arms, for example, which we ethical investors disapprove of, can be used to defend just causes and innocent people under attack. The question is: How do you manage to sell arms only to the nice guys? We all conveniently ignore the vast amounts of money being made in the porn business and get involved with more overt and fashionable causes like deforestation or smoking. We fuss about commercial over-fishing and wink an eye at commercial sex. Do we worry uniformly about the seven deadly sins or are we more selective in our censure? Who chooses, anyway?

There is no doubt that our standards and demands are the ones heeded by our financial experts. But how well informed are we/they? Ethical investors want the "truth," they want "accurate disclosure" about business practices and products. It may be that our designated investors report to us what we want to hear, that they have directed our money toward investments we approve of, ones that represent "fashionable causes" and "scrupulous investments" but ones that are often ethically simplistic. As Peter Hodgson comments, "Who are these people to say that I should not have a glass of wine or a gamble if I wish? Why is South Africa (as it was) listed as the most unethical regime? What about Burma, Libya, China?" He goes on to point out that involvement in nuclear industry "implies that the nuclear industry is totally bad, which is absurd. What about the use of nuclear radiation in medicine? Or nuclear reactors for civil power, arguably the least destructive power source in relation to the environment?"

Most of us would agree that products cannot be morally good or evil in themselves. It's the use people make of them that makes them "bad." Specific moral attitudes, like Puritanism or pacifism or an ecological sense of responsibility induce us to judge something sinful or dangerous or lethal or damaging without reference to the use made of it. These days everyone with a conscience wants to be ethical but it's hard to reduce such complexity to a simple call. Ethical is a nice word. But Dr. Anderson asks, "What has ethical investment to do with ethics? Not much."

Are we caught in a dilemma here? Consider the four main players in the ethical investment business:
- the investment fund companies
- the producer companies in which funds are or are not invested
- the individual investors
- the information groups – watch dogs and auditors.

Got that. Next, consider the list of products and processes that are screened as ethical and unethical, three main groups here:
- arms, gambling and alcohol (the "sin" group)
- healthy planet and animal rights (the "green" group)
- employment conditions.

Of course, if we're going to be really careful, we have to ask if a bank or an investment company itself invests in products we disapprove of. Even when we were so down on South Africa, most of our banks still invested in that country.

You have to examine the bank's reports to know where its money is going. That's just the beginning of your problems. Maybe a company doesn't invest in tobacco. How is it on the environment? Pornography? The list of ethical concerns is a long one. Fuzzy as some of the definitions and distinctions are, here's a list of villains to watch out for:
- armaments
- tobacco
- gambling
- any products (pharmaceuticals, cosmetics) using animal experimentation
- any products using fur obtained by "inhumane" methods[6]
- beers, wines, spirits
- inhumane farming
- involvement in the nuclear industry
- investment in countries with unethical regimes
- failure to promote equal opportunites
- failure to match First World employment conditions in Third World countries[7]

- lack of trade union rights
- inadequate level of charitable giving
- inadequate level of community involvement
- political donations
- unreadiness to disclose information to Ethical Investment (EI) groups
- inadequate health and safety record
- excessive use of greenhouse gases
- use of tropical hardwood
- excessive effluent discharge
- pesticides
- misleading advertising campaigns
- mining.

Some are products; some are processes; some are behavioral problems. The basic question remains the same: how ethical is ethical investment? I do not mean to sound cynical with this question. My heart is usually identified as a bleeding one. I'm just saying that we have to be very sure of what we are doing, have to do a little research on our own, study the facts, be aware of the side effects of some of our actions. The planet we save may be our own.

Whoever said anything was simple?

11

Children's Education

To bring up a child in the way he should go,
travel that way yourself once in a while.
– Josh Billings

The tightwad tycoon, Amy Dacyczyn, may have made a mint with her saving ways, but she and her husband are hanging on to it, she says, because they have six kids to put through college. As I write there is a contest being advertised on TV giving away $10,000 toward a college fund. "How much do you think a university education is going to cost?" an interviewer asks a bunch of kids, and they say "10 dollars" or "50 dollars" or "as much as a car." Then the voice takes over and informs you that four years of university now cost up to $90,000 so you'd better enter this contest and win $10,000. How far is that going to get you? What if you don't win?

The front page banner headline in the *Toronto Star* for August 30, 1997, warns of the effect of increased tuition fees:

FEES CREATE U. OF ELITE

and, "Only rich able to afford university soon, say critics." Inside, on the continued story, the head reads, "Soaring tuition prompts fears education only for the rich," and continues, slightly smaller: "Will money, not brains, govern who is educated?" Maybe it depends on who's using the brains.

This is not a simple problem, nor is it going to go away. Right now, young people are graduating with staggering debt loads that they must pay off before they begin a life. Grants, both individual and to the universities, have dwindled and tuition fees have almost doubled, to the point where 60 percent of Canadian graduates have had to take out loans to pay for their education. Students and their families are scared, too, fearful of that debt load they will saddle themselves with, now standing at $22,000 for a four-year student, expected to reach $25,000 within the next year. The same thing has happened in the United States, with one soothing exception: a bigger system of scholarships, grants and bursaries gives low-income students a better chance to make it. An American graduate of even a private college like Yale will incur about $18,000 in debt.

Postsecondary education used to be a given, a right, and a possibility for anyone whose grades were good enough. My husband put himself through university on the strength of his summer jobs; the year he got fired (for excessive hay fever while lawn-mowing at a golf club), he made his tuition in a judicious week at the races. My own children had a combination of loans and scholarships. During the first couple of years, when grants were higher and my income was smaller, the government looked at my tax return and said, "Here, take money!" to my daughters. They had forgivable loans plus loans they had to pay back after they graduated, with no interest accruing until then. My third child, John, received less in loans and had to earn more summer money than the girls did, but it was possible then, especially, I'm sorry to say, for a boy.[1] Now, with unemployment for young people running as high as 17 percent, it's difficult for anyone, male or female. Even most of the one-fifth of students who do find work are lucky if it's full-time.

I have met 30-something people who are deliberately hiding out from the government in order to avoid paying off their loans with money they still don't have. In fact, the government is carrying a terrible weight of unpaid loans. In 1995 the Canadian government claimed to have lost $61.3 million dollars in defaulted student loans for the previous year alone. For this reason the proposal was made to enact legislation similar to that in the United

States to attempt to cope with the drain. One method is to exempt from bankruptcy discharge any student loan debt for five years after departure from school.

At that time (1995), a student spokesperson claimed that only 3 percent of students were defaulting (to the tune of $60 million?). Since then, with grants down and costs up, students need more money to get through school and then don't make enough money on the jobs available to them after they graduate to enable them to repay the government. They have a choice, they say, between eating and paying off their loans.

A so-called reform recommends that the system of loan payback be geared to a graduate's income, the interest, of course, piling up all the while. The result would be that those who didn't have to start paying until they were earning enough money, would have to pay more because of the accumulated interest – especially hard on women and other visible minorities who still earn less,[2] despite affirmative action. If the interest payments on those loans were tax deductible, that would help.

There's a game called Payday, not as well known as Monopoly but still on the market, that I play with my grandchildren. It teaches the same inexorable lesson that would-be postsecondary students are learning from life: you earn more money if you have a decent education. You'd think governments would understand that people who earn more money pay more taxes. That's too simple. When you cash in your cards at the end of the game, what have you got? Young people in Canada are asking that question and deciding in greater numbers not to go to university, jumping straight into the job market instead. What does that mean to you?

If you are trying to downscale your life, you had better make sure you're not making that decision for your children, although of course if you can teach them what to value, that might help you both. What I'm saying is that as much as you lower your own sights and decrease your expenditures in accordance with less income, don't shortchange your children in the process. There are a few frugal ways and means by which you can help your budding brain surgeon to a university education. The secret is to start yesterday.

If you're a young parent with a bright-eyed baby, you can start right away with an RESP or an in-trust account (see below). If you've waited too long, your child will have to opt for a student loan and hope for a scholarship to help out. Both the feds and the provinces provide student loans, usually between $5,000 and $7,500 per student per year. Once approved as a loan recipient, the borrower must negotiate the details of the loan with a participating bank. Eligibility is usually based on a means test to assess the financial status of both student and family (which is why my girls sailed into their loans; as a recently widowed, single mother I had zilch). Right now, the repayment of the loan is due six months after graduation, with up to ten years to pay. If a graduate can't get a job, the federal government will forgive interest payments for up to 30 months, and something can be worked out with the bank.

I mentioned that my husband financed one year of his university education with winning horses. He never gambled again. No one should count on a horse or a lottery ticket to finance a college education, or anything else.

So, now that we've cleared that up, let's take a good hard look at a Registered Education Savings Plan (RESP), available from most financial institutions (mutual fund and life insurance companies, credit unions, and so on). They are less rigid than they used to be and some are more flexible than others, easily tailored to your and your family's needs. Beneficiaries can be changed should the designated one get ill or decide not to go to university; costs covered can include not only tuition at a recognized institution of learning (usually named in the original designation, but easily transferred), but also anything to do with the postsecondary education in question. This includes room and board, books, transportation, extra tutoring, and so on. Administrative costs are low and you receive regular reports; if the fund your RESP is in doesn't do well, you can transfer it to another more aggressive fund within the company without an additional fee. As the contributor, you can decide not only how the money is to be invested but also how to disperse it. Some plans allow you to contribute CSBs, stocks, bonds, mutual funds or cash, as you choose. Those offered by mutual fund or life insurance companies, being partisan in nature, restrict you to their own products. The lifetime maximum contribution for each beneficiary of an RESP is $42,000 with a ceiling on annual contributions of $4,000. The amounts contributed by you are not tax deductible but they always belong to you; the money earned, tax-free, belongs to the plan. When the beneficiary starts receiving money from it, presumably his or her other income will be so low as not to present a heavy tax problem

One drawback of some RESPs used to be that investment income was forfeited if the beneficiary did not go on to postsecondary education. The earnings went into a pool for others' payouts, typical of a so-called scholarship plan. You could retrieve only your principal, tax-free, of course, because you'd already paid tax on it. Now, however (as of 1998) you can get the investment earnings back under certain conditions. If the beneficiary, 21 years or older, decides not to go on to a "higher" education, and if the RESP is at least ten years old, you can transfer up to $40,000 into your own RRSP or spousal RRSP – but only if you have enough room for it, that is, if you're allowed to contribute that much. Few are. However, you can still take the money, just brace yourself for the tax bite: your marginal rate plus a 20 percent additional tax. Ouch.

Rather than a registered plan, some people prefer a straight in-trust account with your beneficiary's name on it. Note one catch: the donor of the money cannot also be the trustee. (There must be someone you can trust!) Speaking of which, when the child turns 18, the money technically belongs to him or her. I trust that you know your child and that the money will be spent wisely or not at all, that is, that you can keep on administering it for his or her own future good.

With an in-trust account you can be more aggressive and daring while the beneficiary is still young and you have time to recoup if you make a mistake, say for the first 10 years. RESPs must start being disbursed in 20 years, and that's good timing for a trust account too, (keeping in mind your 18-year-old potential maverick). When you get closer to the time that the money may be drawn you can move it into more conservative (safe) funds. About five years away from beginning to use the money, you should collapse about 20 percent of it each year and move the money into GICs, and I do hope the interest rates improve. However, they're not too bad for longer term agreements.

Here's a thought for you. Although young people are normally the beneficiaries, you could easily be the recipient of your own future planning. It's another angle on early "retirement." I mean, when you quit your job you could go back to university yourself or enroll in classes for training that will enable you to support yourself in a different way. The plan's proceeds will give you an income helping to pay for your education costs until your pension or some other investment kicks in. Of course, your taxes will be lower because you will be earning less than in your high-rolling, big-income days.

Education costs are so high these days, and still climbing, that anything you do in the way of an RESP, while good, is likely not going to be enough. It would be nice if you could manage both, RESP and an in-trust account, so that when the time comes, your children can go on to a good, useful, postsecondary education. Maybe some day they'll return the favor and look after you.

Now, what about right now? Somehow or other all systems are go and your kid has started university. Here are a few ways to save tax dollars and lighten the load.[3]

- If you're a parent or grandparent and a business owner, pay your student a salary – low enough so he or she doesn't pay tax but can at least start an RRSP, and high enough that it's a deduction to your business.

- If you own a corporation, lend money to a related student. The loan will be included in the student's income when he/she will pay little or no tax, but this may be deducted later when it is repaid. That deduction could be useful once your student is out there working full-time. Check with your accountant; it gets complicated. If you've simplified your life you're probably not incorporated anyway.

- Even though you're a poor, starving student, file a tax return. Incomes of most students fall below the taxable threshold, usually around $10,000. But a declared income allows you to contribute to an RRSP – 18 percent of any earned income – with room, and deductions, to grow on. Also, a student, 19 years or older, with a declared income, is entitled to receive a refundable GST credit of at least $199 a year. Some provinces even provide a refundable PST credit for low-income taxpayers, including students.

- Claim moving expenses. If the move is at least 40 kilometers and associated with attendance at school or new employment, a student can claim expenses, but not higher than the income earned in the new location.

- Use your RRSP. Maximize contributions, in fact, overcontribute if possible – up to $2,000 is allowed. You don't get the tax credit on the extra money but you do get the tax break on interest earned inside the plan. You say you don't need the deduction because you didn't earn that much money this year? You can save the deduction for a future year when your income is higher (I hope). If you need money, you can take some out without too big a tax hit because you're still so poor.

- Claim the first $500 of any scholarship, bursary, fellowship or prize as tax-free, as allowed by the government. Can you believe it?

- Carry forward or transfer unused tuition and education credits, allowed for the first time in 1997 federal budget. You can use them in a future year.

- Or you can transfer up to $5,000 of these amounts to a spouse, parent or grandparent. Talk to your accountant.

- Repay student loans before investing excess cash. Your interest on a student loan is not deductible. (It should be!)

My kids did that. Liz, the oldest, set the pattern and told her siblings. She put any (briefly) excess money she had into GICs or term deposits, the length of them depending on how soon she figured she needed the money. She earned some interest on her money each year, keeping it as liquid and accessible as she could, spending cash as she needed it, replacing it in interest-bearing instruments as quickly as she could. This small amount of working capital enabled her to pay off her student loan almost as soon as she graduated and started earning money. My kids are smarter than I am, I'm happy to say.

12

Housing

Consider children who don't eat meals together
and don't have to share bathrooms and bedrooms.
They miss an opportunity
to learn interdependence and conflict resolution.
– Doris Janzen Longacre

Shelter is the biggest ticket item anyone has to cover. The traditional financial thinking, according to the Central Mortgage and Housing Corporation (CMHC), is that your payments for shelter, in the case of ownership, should not exceed 35 percent of your gross family income. You'd rest more easily, however, if it were closer to 30 percent of net pay. That's for PIT: Principal, Interest and Taxes. Unexpected and hidden costs can add to the mixed joys of home ownership: legal fees, maintenance, repairs, renovations, heating costs, ever-rising taxes, and so on. The total debt load for a home buyer, according to CMHC, is supposed to be under 42 percent. Those who rent should try to keep their rental expense to between 35 and 50 percent of their total income.

This is often incredibly difficult for poor people to achieve, if not impossible. Obviously there is a price below which landlords will not drop, so that poor people spend a disproportionate amount of their meager income on shelter. When an impossible choice has to be made between shelter and food, more people opt for food banks; the lineups increase as the money intended for food goes to rent payments. When the Harris Government in Ontario slashed welfare payments by 21 percent, the number of homeless increased alarmingly as people could no longer afford to meet their rental payments which were not slashed accordingly. The death rate among them, though conservatively and not accurately[1] counted, comes to about 55 a year in the city of Toronto alone. Michael Shapcott, Communications Officer of the Co-Operative Housing Federation of Canada, who gave me this figure, believes that an estimate of slightly better than one a week is too low and "seriously undercounts the seriousness of the problem." Presumably, you will never have to face the terrible choice between food or shelter.

Why pay rent when you can own? That's the argument of real estate agents who demonstrate the compassionate zeal of social workers as they try to find the right home for their clients. Better, so the conventional wisdom has it, to build equity in a piece of property than to squander nonreturnable funds for a roof that will never be home. Right, up to a point. Some people are just not cut out to be homeowners. They don't want the responsibility of upkeep and taxes. Others want more help than they're getting. Others wonder whether it's possible to share living quarters the way some people are now sharing cars. (Sleep fast, I need the pillow!) Hold that thought.

You who are reading this book are not at subsistence level but perhaps the thought of it will make you pause and take a good long look at your housing choices. We, in North America, tend to take the nuclear family pattern – one family per domicile – for granted and think that is the only way to live. It's probably one of the most expensive designs for living you could find: one roof with one of everything under it, and then when the arrangement breaks down, as almost half of American and one-third of Canadian marriages do, each half of the former couple needs one of everything again, whether supplied in a rental arrangement or purchased for another single-family home setup. The only people who profit by that are the manufacturers of the appliances and furniture and equipment bought on credit, or time. For people who wish to simplify rather than complicate their lives, there are alternatives.

Consider, for example, and we will, briefly, co-operative housing, communal housing, and co-housing. These three very different types of housing have one element in common – some kind of sharing of home and responsibilities. Before your privacy hackles rise up in protest, consider this. Leslie Klein, author of an abstract on Alternative Housing,[2] points out that a sense of community is a feeling many people feel is lost [today]. Some people want it back.

In co-operative housing, owner-occupants live in private self-contained units and share some common elements, such as site, paying for common services (maintenance, repairs, etc.). Members do not own their units as such; they buy membership in the co-operative which entitles them to live in a unit, the size depending on how much the membership cost, or how many shares they purchased, however it's gauged. A board of member-directors manages the incorporated nonprofit business which is conducted for mutual self-help and conducted according to a strict code of ethics. There are about 550 housing co-ops in Ontario alone. The Co-operative Housing Federation of Canada is a nationwide organization concerned right now with lobbying to protect provincial and federal agreements with co-ops.

A number of co-ops in Canada have been formed for the exclusive use of seniors, often low-income. Co-ops often sponsor a home maintenance or home care program within a community.

Communes – popular in the 1960s as part of the nationwide hippie movement – were loosely organized structures, usually rural, very male chauvinistic, as far as I could observe, with the women doing all the work and the men raising the grass.[3] Not too appealing for our needs today.

Co-housing developments (private housing in a communal setting, a form of housing tracing its beginning to 19th-century Europe and revived in Denmark in the 1970s) are gaining in popularity as we come of age. Stressing sustainable living, the in-phrase, every household is a self-sufficient private residence, but also shares larger facilities with the other occupants, such as a big commercial-size kitchen, dining room, workshops and recreation area all suitable for community activities. Transportation shared within the community includes local shuttles, bus service, bicycle paths and private cars with an emphasis on car pooling, and there could be child or elder care and other social services. It sounds a little like a locked community or a retirement village but about 20 of these developments exist now in the US, with 12 more under construction and another 150 in the design stages. These are not necessarily inexpensive solutions, but they simplify life to the extent that people get to share the work in maintaining a home.

In their book *Clicking*, pop megatrend advisor Faith Popcorn[4] and Lys Marigold include a couple of pages about co-housing ("Communal Clanning: Family by Choice"), saying that it is the next big movement, not a mere fad:

> *We think co-housing will Click in the decade and*
> *century ahead...maybe someday*
> *we'll be watching the evening news on Election Night and hear reports*
> *on how the "co-housing vote" is swinging. Because co-housing - and*
> *the tightly knit new Clans it creates – promises to be that big a phenomenon.*

In Kurt Vonnegut's novel *Slapstick*, he describes a presidential election won on the campaign promise, "Lonesome No More." People are arranged into clans by the random selection of a computer program assigning them the names of various flora and fauna. Thus, all the Daffodils are related, and help each other, and have family reunions and so on, and find they have a lot in common. Popcorn's prediction about the clanning effects of co-housing reminded me of the Daffodils. This may be oversimplification, in which case it may be what some people are looking for.

There are, of course, other means of arranging affordable shelter. Many homeowners, whether they're retired, downscaled or unemployed, find that whatever fixed income they have tends to dwindle as they try to keep up with rising costs. There are big-money ways of dealing with this problem (reverse mortgages, co-op housing, etc.). There are also stopgap measures, savvy tricks to save a few bucks on heating. Or you could try a complete change of lifestyle.

Who says you have to own your dwelling place? You may be able to rent an attractive apartment in a good house (with a separate entrance, please) for a fraction of what you'd pay to own it. Depends how old you are; you may no longer want the responsibility for the upkeep of a house. On the other hand, you may be the one who owns the house and rents the apartment to help pay the mortgage or rising taxes. If you're alone, you might offer your services to a homeowner who's too busy or on sabbatical or who travels a lot – whatever – as live-in housekeeper, cook, groundskeeper or security. If part of a couple, offer your joint services as superintendents of an apartment building or a rental unit in a condo in return for reduced or no rent. Twenty-four-hour home care costs a lot these days; you may be able to offer such live-in care in return for a room in an elderly person's large home. In all these cases, I would recommend spelling out the deal and what is expected of each side in a carefully worded contract. It would not be fair to either party to get less than what is being offered.

A few years ago I interviewed a widow with a fixed income who was finding it difficult to keep on living in a huge house in the Back Bay area of Boston because of rising taxes and heating costs. She solved her problem with barter. She let a young couple have the servant's quarters over the garage (that used to be a stable) in return for their cleaning and grounds maintenance and security services. And she let a Japanese couple, both players with the Boston Symphony Orchestra, have a floor of the house in return for their cooking her meals, including the provision of food. (If she tired of Japanese food, she'd ask for a Western-style roast chicken.) She also allowed the couple to use the drawing room as a rehearsal hall for a quartet they played in, on condition that she could bring friends and listen.

I have met several single women in different cities who pooled their resources in order to buy one big house whose expenses they shared, but with separate entrances, kitchens and bathrooms. I have known several informal shared housing arrangements among students, for example, or actors, who share the rent of a large house, take turns cleaning the bathroom (at least, they're supposed to!), and share the cost and cooking of the meals. The combinations and possibilities have only begun to be discovered. Once people lose the ingrained idea of one dwelling/one family, they may come up with some interesting designs for living: cost-sharing, satisfying, simple. Me, I prefer to live alone. There's no accounting for tastes. Some of you, of course, are married or have significant others and prefer larger living quarters, though you wonder how long you can continue to afford them. So take a look at mortgages – granny and reverse. One of these might be for you.

Just last year I ran into an old friend at a reunion and asked her where she was living. With her children, she said, her daughter and son-in-law, in a house. I wondered how that worked, did she pay rent, was she independent, and so on. She said in a very low voice, not to be overheard, "Don't tell. They pay me. I own the house." A granny mortgage!

Not all grannies go with the mortgage. Some live separately and hold the mortgage which a (usually married) child pays into, at attractive but reasonable rates of interest – legal, of course, but helpful to both parties. Some grannies are more informal and hold an honorary second mortgage, simply a generous loan with an open-end payment, often not settled until the will is probated, and the debt, if unforgiven, must be paid into the estate if there are other siblings involved. It really would be best for the sake of all concerned if there is a good, legal paper trail attached to any of these deals.

A reverse mortgage, a much more formal entity, is a financial tool that enables a home owner to turn the equity in the paid-up family home into cash without making mortage payments or selling the house. It's a somewhat risky way for retired people, caught in the squeeze between fixed incomes and rising expenses, to find extra money. However, the advantages often outweigh the risk. Seniors can stay in their own homes longer and stay out of institutions, and they can afford the necessary maintenance on their homes, saving money and consequences down the line. They can also use the money to help their children while they're still around. I recently talked to one senior who told me he had arranged such a mortgage to finance a new business venture his son was undertaking. That's called love!

The danger is, of course, that the reverse mortgage runs out before you do, that is, that the equity gets used up while you're still going strong. Most Canadian companies offering reverse mortgages are quite conservative, however; they won't lend you more than they think you'll last. You both want to be sure there's equity left over. The moral here, as always, is shop around. Don't leap into any agreement too fast. Make sure you know what you're doing. I can give you a few hints, but you'll have to do some extra sleuthing. (They don't call this homework for nothing.)

In a reverse annuity mortgage, you borrow a lump sum on which compound interest will be charged over the life of the mortgage. You use the lump to buy an annuity which gives you monthly payments for life (depending on what kind of annuity you chose. (You really are going to have to read another book.[5]) Your protection here is that even when your home disappears into the reverse mortgage, you still have an annuity to show for it. The current problem is that interest rates on annuities are quite low these days. The good news about this is that you get a monthly income for the rest of your life. You should live so long. On the other hand, it can be expensive, what with compound interest and all. Again, you have to shop around and find the best type of annuity for you. Depending on your age, you may prefer to take out a Registered Retired Income Fund (RRIF), but that's another discussion.

In the meantime, you should also consider a line of credit reverse mortgage. You take your money, but not in a regular dole, using only the amount you need at any given time, like when you need a new roof or a new car or something major, like extra home care after surgery – to a maximum annual amount. You pay interest only on the amount you withdraw. The trick here is to take the money only when you really need it. Don't blow it on foolish extravagant extras.

This can get vicious, especially a fixed term reverse mortgage. Take this in a pinch, while you wait for better days to come. You might have taken early retirement (to a simpler life) and found that you were a little short while waiting for your pension or an investment to cut in, or something or someone to mature (or die?). So you take a reverse mortgage for a fixed term, maybe five, ten years. At the end of the agreed-upon time, you have to pay back the entire amount, plus interest, even if you have to sell the house. Be careful!

For further information you can get a copy of a booklet called *Home Equity Conversion: The Study of Reverse Mortgages as a Housing and Planning Option* (see Appendix 1). In the United States reverse mortgages are available only to those older than 62 years of age, who own their home, with limits based on average home values in the area. In all cases, be aware of concomitant costs, things like appraisal fees, legal expenses and so on, and whether they have to be paid up front and can be charged to the loan. Institutions can be heartless; maybe your kids will stake you to a living in return for the house when you go. You could, of course, consider moving to a smaller home or a condo or even a retirement village. If you manage to make a profit on your sale and spend less on the new arrangements, you'll have some money to invest to keep you functioning happily while you let someone else cut the grass or shovel the snow.

I want to mention a few other money-saving ideas just beginning to be explored: solar homes, geodesic domes, caves.

It has been a myth that solar heating is too experimental and too expensive to be realistic in a Canadian climate. I interviewed the owner of a house in Bracebridge, Ontario, (225 kilometers north of Toronto) where the winters are cold, long and dark, who heated his house successfully with solar heat and saved money. A neighbor a few doors down on my lake not only has solar heating panels on his roof but heats the place with a heat pump water system which I don't begin to understand. A couple in Richmond, BC, report that they built and live in a geodesic dome and find it beautiful, strong, easy to maintain and warm, costing about 40 percent less to heat and cool because it has 30 percent less surface area exposed to the outside. Another couple report from Indiana that they have built a 20th-century cave, a dwelling set into a hill and covered with earth except for the south side, warmer in winter and cooler in summer, light and dry and heated with only a fireplace.[6]

The Alberta Sustainable House may make converts of us all. Architects Org and Helen Ostrowski and Orian Low of ASH Inc. (Autonomous and Sustainable Housing Inc.) built the house to prove that it's possible to enjoy the customary suburban comforts independent of city services such as gas, electric, water and sewer lines, and with little or no strain on Earth's resources. In fact, much of the building material was recycled: floors from recycled glass; insulation from pulverized newspapers; interior partitions from a building being taken down. The innovations and techniques are wondrous but what concerns us most here is the cost. With the support of companies, sponsors and individuals, the house was financed with a conventional mortgage. Estimates are that the savings on utilities will be about $1,300 a year, and more, as costs keep going up. Sustainable Houses may be the homes of the future. ASH Inc. hopes to build an entire community of them in the city of Calgary.

In Doris Janzen Longacre's posthumous book, *Living More with Less*, friends wrote in to add to what she didn't have time to finish. But in a brief, powerful introduction to a consideration of homes, Longacre suggests most importantly that this world is not our home, that consciously or not, we are all heading for another Home that awaits us. That's why it's important for us to remember that home has "more to do with friends and love than with expansive family rooms."

Longacre urges adaptation: improving the insulation, for example, in order to stay on in an old house near school and work, while saving energy and money at the same time; acceptance: "you don't change houses like you give up plastic wrap or switch to a smaller car"; and retrofitting: making do by adding a solar system or double-paned glass, putting more people in a too-big house; organizing a small house; insulating a cold one and wearing long underwear, shutting off rooms in winter, adding awnings for summer.

"Retrofitting," writes Longacre, "means trying to live now the way we should, rather than waiting for the big event that will make it easy to do so."

That sounds simple.

13

Cars

Assume there were a technological breakthrough that would allow people to travel as easily and cheaply between continents as between nearby cities. Unfortunately, there would also be 100,000 deaths a year from the device. Would you try to prevent its use?[1]
– Gregory Stock

By the time we had four busy children it was evident we needed a second car just to make sure they kept all their appointments and attended all their lessons. I felt really affluent with my own car, just like Mrs. Ladidah Suburbia, but the car rapidly turned into a plow. In addition to driving my own kids I was also doing chauffeur duty for others and I became the designated driver who picked up the shirts and returned the library books and dropped in to visit my mother, "on my way by," and took her shopping and did her errands too. My husband stopped phoning just before he left work to see if I needed anything because he knew I was driving the plow and could get it myself. That's when I learned that cars cause more work.

By the time I was alone and living in a downtown apartment in Toronto close to a subway line, I realized that if I stayed on in the city I would probably get rid of the car. In fact, when I went to buy a new one I let the company take possession of my old car immediately and went without for three months while I waited for the new year's models to come in. I took the subway, walked, took taxis when necessary, and that, during a horribly busy period when one of my children had major surgery and I had a new play open and a book tour starting. Just think what I saved in parking expenses!

Living where I do now, ten kilometers from the nearest store, I need a car for everything I do and I apologize. Grocery shopping, banking, mailing letters, t'ai chi in another town, entertainment (the video store), meetings, work and visits to my children in Toronto are all dependent on fossil fuel. I can walk one kilometer to the restaurant down on the highway for a beer with friends – not very often. (I don't have many friends.) The simplest solution would be not to go anywhere, which I'm working on, but it's not always possible while I am still hustling for a living. I am just not ready to walk 200 kilometers into Toronto to meet with a publisher. Mind you, the publisher of this book lives four provinces away. We never use the car to communicate, not while we have phone, fax and E-mail. The times are changing.

If I were living in the city now, I think I would share a car. Canadian author Joy Kogawa told me that's what she does now. She sold her car to a car-share place in Vancouver and uses it when she needs it. Tracey Axelsson of the Co-operative Auto Network (CAN) sent me lots of information and reminded me of Thoreau's attitude to mechanical travel.

"I have learned," wrote our hermit, "that the swiftest traveller is he that goes afoot."

He supposes a situation where he and a friend will try to reach a destination some 30 miles away, one on foot, one by train, to see who gets there first. The fare is 90 cents, almost a day's wages in those days. The writer says he can start on foot and easily arrive that night while his friend must work first to earn his fare and will get there the next day or evening, if he has been able to get "a job in season." Thoreau would beat him.

"And so," he concludes, "if the railroad reached around the world, I think that I should keep ahead of you." The interesting point is that he equates the cost of travel to the time one has to work to pay for it – a variation of Dominguez and Robin's life-energy line. Brother, can you spare the time?

"Better Transportation: Getting rid of our gridlock, pollution and debt," reads the headline on the complete information available on the first Web site in the world to explain car sharing (see Appendix 1). The only four co-ops operating in North America are in Quebec City, Quebec (Auto-Com), with 200 members and 20 cars; Montreal, Quebec (CommunAuto, same management); the CAN in Vancouver; and a satellite co-op in Victoria, British Columbia (Victoria Car Share Co-op). Another idea whose time has come, in Canada there are groups forming as I write in Ottawa and Toronto, Ontario; and Edmonton, Alberta; in the United States: Portland, and Corvallis, Oregon; Seattle, Washington; San Francisco, California; Boulder, Colorado; and maybe Boston, Massachusetts. A Station Car (a car that runs with a credit card insert) is proto-testing at a university in California. Check and see, and join the car-sharing listserv to discover ways and means of establishing organized car-sharing initiatives.

The latest estimate of the cost of owning and running a car in a city is about $7,000 a year, or higher, depending on the make of the car, and factoring in car payments, gas, oil, repairs, washes, license, insurance (according to the price of the car),[2] and parking. Tests have proven over and over that it costs less to take transit or taxis or other people out of their way than it does to own a car.

The first (weak) argument against getting rid of your car is, what do you do when it rains and cabs dissolve? And of course, you find it much more pleasant to be alone with your thoughts and a disc jockey than jostling people in a crowded bus or go-train.

But think of what you're doing to the environment when you drive, and to your own stress levels. A new hazard has emerged on highways now, something called road rage, the often lethal anger of other motorists who endanger the lives of or even kill a driver who annoys them. Then, too, fossil fuels keep going up in price and the high cost of parking is enough to give anyone an aching wallet. For all these reasons you should consider alternate, cheaper means of going from Point A to Point B. (Failing a pair of sparkling red shoes with heels to click, I'm looking forward to telekinesis.)

Commercial rental cars are, of course, available; travelers use them in other cities and carless motorists enjoy them for out-of-town visits. But for regular use in a city, the costs add up, despite the lure of frequent flyer points. Car sharing affords drivers low-cost access to a car without burdening them with the whole debt load or the bother and expense of maintenance. The cost structure is quite easy and varies according to the plan chosen: regular, weekender, or car-free. All insurance and gas costs and PST/GST are included in the monthly administration fee (yearly for the car-free or occasional driver), with a set hourly charge and x cents per kilometer depending on how much you drive. The real thrill is that there's never anything wrong with the car. Maintenance is constant and prompt. Members are allowed to switch categories as their needs change. Reports already coming in reveal substantial savings which, of course, are going directly into RRSPs or mutual funds!

CAN manager Axelsson admits that car sharing is not for everyone. "It takes trust, a certain level of flexibility and a real commitment to using alternative means of getting around." It also means that you are doing something tangible for the environment, using cars only as a last resort; for your community, not crowding your city streets, putting less stress on air and space. You'll probably do yourself a physical as well as a financial favor, too, by walking more. Remember walking?

Just in case you're wondering about those monstrous car costs, Axelsson offers this calculator to help you assess them.[3] If you take the time to figure this out, you'll find it's an eye opener.

FIXED COSTS

EXPENSE ITEM	COST	
Value of your car	Purchase Price _____	(A)
	Trade-in Value _____	(B)
Depreciated value (Subtract the trade-in value from the purchase price and divide by the number of years you expect to own the vehicle)	$(A - B) \div X =$ _____	(C)
Insurance	_____	(D)
Taxes	_____	(E)

License and Registration   _____ (F)

Finance Charges   _____ (G)

TOTAL FIXED COSTS   C + D + E + F + G   _____ (1)

VARIABLE COSTS PER YEAR

Fuel Costs

Gas and oil per kilometer (use the manufacturer's specs)   x   Number of kilometers driven

City = _____/km x _____ (i)   = _____ (H)

Highway = _____/km x _____ (ii)   = _____ (I)

TOTAL FUEL COSTS   H + I   = _____ (2)

ASSOCIATED COSTS PER YEAR

Maintenance (AirCare, oil changes, repairs, brakes, warranty, servicing, etc.) _____ (J)

Tires   _____ (K)

Other costs (car washes, roadside assistance, etc.)   _____ (L)

TOTAL ASSOCIATED COSTS   J + K + L = _____ (3)

TOTAL CAR COST

TOTAL FIXED COSTS (1)   _____

TOTAL FUEL COSTS (2)   _____

TOTAL ASSOCIATED COSTS (3)   _____

TOTAL CAR COST   (1 + 2 + 3)   _____ (4)

TOTAL CAR COST PER KILOMETER

Total car costs (4) _____ ÷

number of kilometers driven (i + ii) _____

TOTAL CAR COST PER KILOMETER   =   _____

We'll see what happens to this trend as the price of cars and gas keeps escalating and as people worry more about nonrenewable resources and the greenhouse effect. In the meantime, the majority of people in North America who drive prefer to own their own car. Making inroads, however, on car purchase figures are the lease figures. More and more people, short of cash, preferring a new car on a regular basis, or self-employed (which gives them the best tax deal), are leasing instead of buying a new car. I'm one of them. There's a simple rule here: buy a car in December, lease a car in January. You get a year's worth of depreciation on a December purchase and a year's worth of receipts on a January lease, that is, if you're self-employed and need the car for your business.

What about second-hand cars? Forget the little old lady who drove the car only on Sundays to go to church, you must be very very careful when buying a used car. (Put that car down! You don't know where it's been!) Here's a neat rule of thumb Tracey Axelsson gave me: If the vehicle is more than five years old, you will repay the sticker price of the car within two years with maintenance bills.[4] Nevertheless, there is a time and need for a second-hand car, especially when it is the second car in a family, or third or fourth.

Friends of mine in Iowa who own two cars (actually, one is a company car) wanted a third car for their son when he was ready to go off to college, mainly because they wanted him to be able to come and visit on weekends. My friend Patty Stilwill told me how she went about her shopping. First, she read a couple of paperback books on how to buy a used car.

Patty learned enough to look knowledgeable and you can too. There are some basics anyone can do. When she went for the test drive, she started the car and then tried everything – windshield wipers, lights, turn signals, air conditioning, heating – and didn't say a word. Silence makes salesmen nervous. Hers started talking, saying what shocks the car had, what a smooth ride it gave and so on, repeating himself. She simply didn't say anything and let him dig a hole with his mouth.

During the drive, she did everything she could think of to test the car's response: sudden braking, sharp turns, swift acceleration, changing lanes, etc. He thought she was a terrible driver. When they stopped, she asked to look under the hood. She says she didn't know much but she knew the difference between the transmission fluid and the oil. She looked at the stick for the fluid and asked for a cloth to wipe it clean to check; it's supposed to be a clear reddish color. The salesman asked if she wanted to check the oil.

"This is the transmission," she said.

"Looks okay to me," he said.

"It looks murky," she said, and went on to check the oil.

He got more nervous, and that's when he started in about the shocks. He leaned on one side; it didn't sound too good.

"Well, that side is a little soft," he admitted, "but it's good, might have to be checked down the line." He leaned on the other side. "This side's fine. Good shocks," he said again.

Patty went over and leaned on the side he said was fine. She's a fair-sized lady and the car protested. She told me at that point she didn't know what she was doing, but was just copying his actions. When the car begrudged her, the salesman got more nervous.

That's when she told him she'd been reading a book.

"What color?" he asked, suddenly very nervous. The fact that she might have seen a price list in a book like our red book or blue book, reporting used car evaluation and price lists, seemed to strike fear in the heart of the salesman.

What Patty noticed with every dealership she went to, shopping around, was that the salesman in each case had a sale in mind for her, something he wanted to unload and pushed like mad. In no case would the salesman come down in price, even when she asked directly, "What's the rock bottom price?" Here is where women buyers must beware more than men. Several investigations have proved that women pay up to $500 more for a car, on average, than men.

The comedienne Emily Levine has a routine about women's troubles with car repairs, or rather, with garage mechanics.

"They look at you like you're stupid and they say, 'It's a gasket, honey.' Like I don't know what a gasket is. I know what a gasket is. A gasket is $150. A 'gasket, honey' is $200."[5]

My friend Stilwill got a very good deal on a second-hand car. You can too, with a little homework. It's simple when you know how.

14

The High Cost of Dying

To church; and with my mourning, very handsome,
and new periwig, make a great show.
– Samuel Pepys, March 21, 1667

If we're going to be consistent about this simple approach to life, I think we had better consider the high cost of dying. Simple-minded people have trouble coming to terms with the fact of their own or a loved one's death. You'll save yourself and/or your survivors a lot of angst and probably quite a bit of money if you take the time to make a few arrangements in advance.

Funerals can be very expensive but they need not be as pricey as you fear if you plan ahead. That way you or your family won't be vulnerable to the emotional blackmail so easily dumped on the recently bereaved. I don't want to malign undertakers; they have a hard job and most of them perform it with dignity and compassion. But they're selling a product and they can't be blamed for trying to make a little extra money. So some of them try to appeal to your emotions, especially guilt, but also pride, to persuade you to go for the classier casket and all the trimmings of a big-time sendoff. As my father said, when he suggested (before he died, obviously) that we not go overboard on the price of the box, "I'm only going to use it once." I tried to get a cheaper coffin for my husband but the funeral director phoned me after I'd returned home from that sad shopping expedition to inform me that Bill was too tall to fit into what I had chosen and I'd have to go for a Tall Model, like his pajamas. I didn't know then what I know now.

By the time my mother died I had joined a memorial society who helped me to a crematorium. In that case I paid only for transfer services, which involved the transporting of the body from the place of death (the hospital) to the crematorium and the handling of all necessary legal documentation. I put the box containing my mother's ashes into a shoulder tote bag and flew her back to my father's plot in Winnipeg where her church gave her a memorial service and one of my best friends had a reception following. Since then I have discussed my own arrangements with my children. We have agreed that if I die in another country on a trip, they are not to attempt to bring my body back because a one-way trip in cargo is too expensive. Let me be planted where I fall. On the other hand, there is still a place waiting for me beside my husband's grave in Stratford and it would be a shame to let it go to waste. If it's convenient, they can carry my ashes there, or strew them on my lake if it's not. I don't suppose I'll notice the difference.

Anyway, I pass on to you a few tips[1] which you can choose to use or ignore:

- Generic funerals cost between $3,000 and $5,000 now. Think about it.
- The average markup on caskets runs from 200 to 400 percent.
- Shopping after the fact is painful. Get recommendations from family or friends.
- Get a price list, which funeral homes are legally required to provide.
- It will not surprise you to learn that prices vary.
- Arrangements can be made in advance to donate your body to a medical school for teaching purposes. Usually the university will arrange for burial but don't count on acceptance; make alternative arrangements.
- Donor cards for the donation of tissue or organs[2] are available from funeral directors. Most provinces now have a space on their driver's licence for you to sign, indicating what you are willing to donate.

- It is illegal for a funeral director to say a particular casket or container will protect a body better than any other.
- Embalming is not required by law unless the body is to be transported and more than 72 hours have elapsed since death or since the removal of the body from refrigerated storage.
- Grave liners are not legally required, though some cemeteries prefer them.
- Memorial services at the funeral home are optional. If you have a close religious affiliation, you may prefer to have a service at your church, temple or synagogue.
- "Viewing the body" – a visitation at the funeral home the day or evening before the service is popular in some regions of the country. (That's where they get the expression *Slumber Room*. "Mrs. Soandso is in Slumber Room B.")
- Cremation averages between $1,500 and $2,000.
- Coroners usually require that cremation not take place before 48 hours from the time of death. (This gives other members of the family a chance to protest, or, in the event of suspicious circumstances surrounding the death, to give the police a chance to examine the body.)
- Pre-cremation caskets are not necessary if there is to be no viewing. This option is called *direct cremation*.
- It is not necessary to buy a special urn for the ashes; they will be packaged in a plain cardboard box.
- Offer the mourners an alternative to flowers with a suggestion of the charitable organization of your choice.

If you are intent on saving money and hassle at the time of a death, it would be a good idea to join a Memorial Society ahead of time. A Memorial Society is "a non-sectarian, non-profit consumer group dedicated to simplicity, dignity and economy in funeral rites," what I call a Last Call Price Club. There are 25 chapters in every province of Canada, with the exception of New Brunswick and Prince Edward Island (see Appendix 1). Cost of a one-time membership fee runs from $10 to $35.

For this you usually get:

- a membership card
- a final arrangements form to specify your pertinent data and choices
- one copy of a *Living Will* [3]
- a list of medical schools and how to contact them
- a list of local co-operating funeral homes and a price comparison
- a Vital Information Record form
- a regular or irregular newsletter, if your chapter has one.

If you want to carry your planning one step further, in some provinces (Ontario, for one) you can even prepay your funeral, purchasing it at today's prices. The money is put into trust, earning interest, until it's used; if there's any left over, it goes into your estate. My worry would be the same as my worry about a cryogenic interment (body frozen until further notice): what if the company goes out of business? Where does that leave me? In the case of a preplanned but unpaid funeral, the price agreed upon at the time of selection is paid at the time of death by the estate. Remember, if you live too long, inflation and other costs may cause the price to rise above the original quoted amount. You may not care.

I recently read of a couple of interesting solutions for coping with the remains. Some famous people in the United States, including the LSD guru Timothy Leary, had their ashes flown into outer space – quite ethereal, not to say out of this world. And *Marvel Comics* editor Mark Gruenwald had his ashes mixed in with the ink during the printing of a comic book. He lives on in the pages of a reissue of *Squadron Supreme*.

Do not go simply into that good night.

15

Frugal Is as Frugal Does

Spare no expense to make everything
as economical as possible.
– Samuel Goldwyn

Brace yourself. For many people, this chapter will be the heart of the matter: how to save money and be happy; tips for the tightwad and the financially challenged. It may well be the last self-help list you'll ever need, a generic guide to coping forever. Your purpose is to de-junk your life, get rid of the clutter, and oh, yes, save the planet while you're at it. I am about to offer you a bouquet of tightwad tips, a nosegay of cheapskate ideas, an armful of moneysaving methods. You can take them or leave them. To some people lists are like mother's milk. Others prefer gin. My one piece of advice to the reluctant list-reader is to skip this chapter.

One other thing before we begin this assault. Do try to remember the difference between saving and savings. You can save a few quarters on the judicious use of coupons – some people claim to save as much as $10 every shopping day – or you can catch a good sale on pantyhose or get your film developed more cheaply, but where is the money you saved? Gone. Never there in the first place, unless you stashed it somewhere. If you're serious about saving money and putting the money you save to good use, then be sure you make that your goal. You want to see tangible results. If you can manage to save $500 a month in your all-out attack on the cost of high living, then invest the money and make it work for you. Eventually you won't have to make as much because you'll be living on your interest/dividends.

Unless you're really into the simplicity movement, you're going to find it uphill work to fight the traffic pattern. Most people are still in the buying mode. Even when the economy slumped, it wasn't because Canadian consumers didn't want to buy things; they didn't have the money. Actually, what they were buying was mutual funds, those who were still employed but fearful for their jobs and future. I certainly don't want to undermine the economy by recommending that we accelerate this save-now-buy-later trend. If we all did it we'd put people out of business and hurl the entire country into a neverending downward spiral. Still, it wouldn't hurt any of us to stop before we splurge, think before we indulge, look before we leap into a credit-card-busting, spending frenzy. You can begin easily enough with thoughtful, informed shopping, scouting the sales, using your coupons, thinking laterally (making one product do the work of three or four), doing without, swapping. However, let's start with the big-ticket items.

Heat and Power

You have already settled in your dream home and you're happy. Now you want to keep it warm. I remember my father pointing out people who were not afraid of what the neighbors thought, who banked their small houses with earth or sod to keep in the heat. We didn't live in that section of the city. I'm talking Winnipeg winters here. You might not bury your house, but you could add extra insulation. If you can't afford new, airtight storm windows, try covering them with heavy plastic sheeting in the winter. Every fall Ontario Hydro sends out a bulletin telling customers how to cut their heating costs. The simplest way is to stop heat from leaking out. You don't want to heat the whole outdoors. So close all the holes in the house, chinks and fissures and air spaces.

My cottage was on stilts at the front as the ground slopes under it down to the lake. All the winds in Ontario blew under my floor, cooling my feet. I had the space enclosed, the result being an odd, insulated, multilevel room, each level resting on bedrock wherever the builder met it – better than using dynamite under my house. This add-under gave me a firm support for my filing cabinets and additional space for a washer and dryer, which are not very ecological, but I have no desire to pound clothes at the edge of an icebound lake. It also cut the heating bills, I think.

I blew more insulation into the house to save heat. I built those walls under the house to save heat. I wrapped my hot water tank to save heat. I guess if I hadn't done those things I'd be paying more. As it is, I'm not paying less. I hope I'm saving money. See what I mean about the difference between saving and savings?

The trick, as I've discovered, is to keep my body warm and not the whole house. I live and sleep in the front of the house overlooking the lake with a view of the stars. In the winter I turn off the heat in the bedrooms, each with its separate heater, and shut the doors. I put those long quilted, wormy things, stuffed dachshunds or cats with long tails, on the floor along the doors so the cold air doesn't seep in. I also put one on the floor against the stove so the outside vent designed to carry off cooking odors doesn't blow cold air back in. I sleep on my futon (on a frame; it looks like a sofa by day) near the fireplace, in a flannelette nightgown with a flannelette-covered duvet. (I don't slide much). Very cosy. But just in case, I warm up the bed with a little heating pad before I get in. That way I can turn the thermostat way down at night.

About the fireplace. I haven't done it yet but I know I'll have to soon, and that is put an insert in the space, and probably choose pellets to burn rather than wood. It's an ethical decision I have been putting off because I love the aesthetics of a fire. There is no doubt that there are other sources of heat that we all should consider. Years ago I did a couple of articles for *Homemaker's* magazine about saving money, appealing to readers to write in. One of the biggest savings they reported was in switching to wood stoves for their heating. Year-round neighbors where I live tell me they can heat their entire (small) houses with the heat from a fireplace equipped with an insert. On the other hand, if everyone did this, we'd be polluting the atmosphere with smoke. In the city, in larger homes, switching to gas will lower heating costs, as will installing a fuel pump in the basement of really large homes, to circulate the hot air? water? more efficiently. Most heating/cooling experts will tell you to moderate your needs. In the winter, be a little cooler and in the summer, a little warmer. Set your thermostats at a more temperate, cheaper, degree. If you're cold, put on a sweater or do some exercises to get your blood circulating rather than that expensive heated air. If you're hot, slow down, think cool thoughts, drink some water, run through the hose.

Even hotels now ask you to turn off the lights when you leave your room. You can do that at home. Even hotels ask you to think twice before you toss a towel, barely used. Even hotels ask you if you'd mind having your sheets changed every other night instead of every night, if you're staying longer than three nights. You can do all that at home. People didn't use to wash so much, still don't, in other countries or continents. The ad agencies decided how much we should wash because they wanted us to buy their clients' products, all the soaps and detergents and bleaches and softeners designed to keep us squeaky clean and terribly busy, not to say overworked. In pioneer times, even a century ago, wash day was only once a week, maybe once a month. In earlier centuries than that, Wash Day was staged once or twice a year. I'm not recommending it; I'm just reporting. Before I had space for a washer and dryer in my semi-basement, I had the best-traveled laundry in Ontario. I became a connoisseur of Laundromats. Unlike other travelers who leave home with clean clothes, I'd take my dirty ones with me and wash when I reached my destination. But to go longer between wash loads, I needed more underwear – cheaper than the gas and time required to get to a washing machine. Even my closest Laundromat was 25 kilometers distant. The point is, don't let your laundry run your life. Be clean but not sterile.

Same goes for the use of water. I learned in Bermuda (where I used to go to write before I had my own retreat), from my hosts there, to shower by wetting my body, turning off the water while I soaped down, then turning it on again to rinse. Same routine with tooth brushing. Taking my water from a lake as I do now, I'm not as careful; I must admit that in the winter I do stand blissfully under running hot water. We are aware now from recent public warnings that people don't wash their hands frequently or carefully enough. The secret lies in the soap, not the water, and time – up to a minute. You do not want to pass on the salmonella.

Experts are also warning us about mites, those awful little creatures invisible to the naked eye that crawl all over your face eating your dead skin, and isn't it a good thing, because I wouldn't want to.[1] That's why you launder your sheets and pillowcases, to get rid of the mites, and I'm glad and be sure to keep them to yourself. Just as we agree with the saying, different strokes for different folks, so we follow the rule, different mites for different nights. Change the sheets for other people. If you feel you're doing too much laundry, and using too much water and power, stop having overnight guests.

If you must use a dishwasher, at least wait until you have a full load. My friends in Bermuda told me that the power company on the island asked everyone to cut down on their usage. People put in ceiling fans and turned off their air conditioners; they hung their clothes out to dry instead of using their dryers; they stopped using their dishwashers or, if they did use them, waited until they were jam-packed and then turned them off after the rinse cycle and opened the door to let the dishes air dry without heat. The savings were so spectacular that the power company couldn't meet its budget and slapped a surcharge on all households. There must be a moral there somewhere.

Equipment

I reviewed all the stuff you need in a kitchen quite recently in my cookbook for singles,[2] so I'm not going to do it again, because I think that many of my precepts apply equally to people in a family or group. Unless you're a dedicated and gifted gourmet cook you don't need three-quarters of the gadgets and equipment offered so temptingly in kitchen stores, and even then I'd want to know how often you make pots de crème or cornucopias or terrines or demi-glace to justify your buying the equipment. I think we should have lending libraries for seldom-used equipment, and not only for the kitchen. In the meantime, buy sparingly and think laterally. I haven't used a garlic crusher since my son showed me how to use the flat of a big knife.

A food processor is useful; a pasta machine not so, unless your grandmother is Italian. Bread machines strike me as an unnecessary luxury. Kneading dough is one of the most acceptable ways there is of getting rid of unexpressed hostility. You can slap dough around without hurting anyone. A freezer is very useful, even the small one on top of your refrigerator, and so is a microwave oven, a stripped-down model that doesn't take up too much room on your counter. Both of them are great for leftovers. Leftovers are required eating when it comes to saving money.

You must discipline yourself not to throw good money after bad. In the kitchen, don't throw away good food, and don't let it go bad. Here, finally, I can offer you a generic list.

Shopping (food)

- Plan your meals.
- Make a list.
- Shop from your list and stick to it.
- Don't take the kids shopping, if you can help it,
  or your husband, if you are the designated shopper (female).
- Don't shop when you're hungry.[3]
- Shop specials for the best buys.
- Buy produce in season.
- Use coupons, but only if you really use the product.
- Try to shop for at least a week at a time.
- If you run out between trips, walk don't drive to the closest convenience store but remember things cost more there.
- Observe Canada's Food Rules.
- Don't buy junk food (unbuttered popcorn or pretzels are the lowest fat, best nutrition).
- Read the labels, not just for fat and calorie content, but for unit price. Bigger is not always cheaper.

- Buy generic or store brands, but make sure they really are less expensive.
- Stop eating meat, or at least cut down. You'll save money and lower your fat intake.
- Cook food from scratch. I know you're busy but the food you prepare at home is much much cheaper – and better-tasting!
- Make your own baby food, easy with a food processor. Freeze it in individual ice cube containers.
- Experiment with new, cheaper foods, like beans and lentils, couscous, bulgur, and of course, pasta in all its different forms. Poorer countries have delicious and inexpensive solutions to your daily eating challenge.
- You don't need to buy a new cookbook (what am I saying?!). Read the labels. Go to the library.

Then there are all those products that can be bought in a grocery store but that aren't food: all the miracle cleansers that lighten up your work load, clean up your home, and mess up the (choose one) landfill, water table, ozone layer. Housewives have known for ages the wonders you can perform with inexpensive items found in any home: vinegar, lemon juice, soda water, toothpaste, and baking soda.

Here's a list, that I copied from an ad, of some of the health complaints you can treat with baking soda, give or take a few other ingredients: sore gums, canker sores and sunburn; sore throat; heartburn and acid indigestion; bee stings and blisters; psoriasis; acne and poison ivy; stuffy nose and itchy eyes; lost salt from diarrhea; vaginal itching; athlete's foot.

The ad continues with a list of cleaning products you can make with baking soda recipes: bleaching formula; scouring powder; drain cleaner; dishwasher detergent; oven cleaner; allergy-free deodorizers; upholstery cleaner; rust remover; tile cleanser; cleaner for gold, silver and pearl jewelry; denture soak.[4]

These are not the only household remedies that you'll find out there. Similar tips abound in all the thrifty newsletters that have sprung up in the wake of *The Tightwad Gazette*. Home methods are a favorite subject on Home Pages.

As for household amenities, like candles, napkins, paper plates (bad for the ecology), baskets, and so on, go to the kitsch stores or the discount houses and buy in bulk. The Price Club or some local variant does not always offer the best bargain in town. I often pick up lowerpriced toilet paper, light bulbs, coffee, popping corn and instant soups (for travel) when I go to a discount office supply store for my stick pens, paper, notepads, sticky notes, cellulose tape and printer cartridges.

Buy your cosmetics in the drugstore and avoid the high prices that come with luxurious packaging and glamorous lettering. I read somewhere that a thin layer of Crisco will do as much for your skin as most of the age-erasing creams you pay so much for. I use Nivea Creme myself. Twenty-five years ago I read that if you lie on your back when you sleep you won't get as wrinkled as you would lying on your side or stomach, so I turned over. I have no quality control to show what I'd look like if I hadn't done this, but I figure I've saved a face lift. (Humor me.) Generic drugs don't cost as much if you're not worried about losing the control that brand names claim they give you. Am I telling you anything you don't already know?

Shopping (clothes, other)

- Make garage sales a way of life (also a source of entertainment!).
- Remember that junking is now considered sport shopping.
- Shop nearly-new stores and sell to them as well, if they'll even look at your old nearly-new clothes.
- Shop discount stores. (I don't have to tell you any of this.)
- Shop thrift stores: Salvation Army, Good Will, Junior League. They will all yield bargains if you know what to look for. I heard of someone who bought a volunteer's new winter coat from one of the good-hearted ditzy clerks at a Junior League Thrift Shop.
- Women, shop the boys' and men's wear departments for cheaper sweaters, Tees, and Oxford cloth shirts.

- Buy a good pair of barber's scissors and do your family's hair. Go to a hairdressing school offering your head for a student to practice on. It takes courage but it's a lot cheaper than designer styling. You could always grow your hair.

Big Ticket Items
(cars, appliances, furniture, and toys)

- Keep on thinking laterally. You can boil water just as easily in a saucepan as in a kettle, unless you're an absent-minded writer and need an electric kettle that will shut itself off when you forget to come back. If you need a kettle, check the garage sales first. I found a brand-new one for $5 at a sidewalk sale in Westmount. Note: the better the neighborhood, the bigger the bargain. I even know someone who bought a Cadillac at a garage sale.
- I knew a very wealthy woman who bought a pair of beat-up upholstered chairs at the Good Will and then had them re-covered – at great expense. At the price of reupholstering these days it's usually cheaper to buy new. This is the price of the terrible (planned?) obsolescence and the high cost of labor that causes good stuff to end up in landfill.

Amy Dacyczyn, as I have already acknowledged, is the queen of the tightwads. She launched her *Tightwad Gazette* newsletter in 1990, followed by three books, *The Tightwad Gazette*, volumes I, II, and III ($12.99 US), each offering collections of tips and penny-pinching ideas gathered from the now defunct monthly publication. In seven years, Dacyczyn and her husband, Jim, with a combined income of $30,000, paid off their debts, bought two new cars, new household appliances, and saved almost $50,000 cash for a down payment on a new house. Now with the bestselling books giving them a six-figure income, Dacyczyn is still counting her cash because the couple has six children to put through college. She says that cutting corners is her way of life and "besides, I'm a role model for a lot of people."

The *Tightwad Gazette* is a role model for a lot of magazines, too, over 30 at last count, all offering simple ways to save big money. One of the newer ones, *Savvy Discounts*, claims that a family can save $5,000 a year with no extra work and no change in lifestyle, and "every dollar saved is tax-free income. It's like giving yourself a tax-free pay raise."

For real savings, you can shop the dumpsters. I have read two detailed articles about dumpster diving which serve as commentary on our wasteful society. One, by Dirk Jamison, was reprinted in the *Utne Reader* from the *L.A. Weekly* in 1996.[5] The writer described his father's forays into trashing. The man stumbled onto it by accident when, out of work, he found an old beggar sitting in a dumpster eating cold spaghetti from a can and offering to share his "score" of chicken, broccoli, mangoes, a mystery novel and a bag of hard candy. The chicken was tightly wrapped, freshly tossed, and didn't come any cheaper. Jamison's dad developed a technique and made the same discoveries about dumpster food as the other reporter I read. Store managers will throw out a carton of eggs if one egg is cracked; boxes of cereal if one corner is crushed; day-old bagels and other baking (though sometimes smaller stores will sell these for a lower price); cartons of yogurt or cottage cheese past their use-by dates – by one day; slow-selling trail mix or unpopular flavors of potato chips; bananas or mangoes with blemishes (also often sold marked down); other different kinds of overripe fruit. Jamison's parents divorced, as much over where they shopped, I gather, as anything else. Once his father took off for Mexico and reported that trash there was really trash.

The better the neighborhood, the better the scavenging. We in the First World produce very good garbage. It may repel you to scrounge for food in a dumpster (it does me), but one man's poison is another man's meat. I do know people who regularly patrol dumpsters for other material. A friend of mine found a year's supply of party napkins and paper plates and a collection of Valentine card booklets in a dumpster a stationery store had filled with old stock (but new goods) before relocating. To an avid scrounger, more trash means more cash.

To some people, all this activity sounds like a lot of work, and rather distasteful at that. To others, it offers all the excitement of the chase and the glee of the successful catch. A lot of people find it enjoyable, that's why they keep on doing it. No one is smugger than someone who has just saved a bundle, made a deal, found a bargain, and somehow, therefore, beaten the odds and come out ahead. Most people don't make something like this a habit unless they think it's fun.

Housework

The one thing nobody thinks is fun is housework. Our esteemed patron saint of feminism, Gloria Steinem, calls housework "shitwork," and no one argues with her. What you have to do is simplify your approach. Here are a few thoughts designed to ease your conscience, lighten your load, and put some spring back in your cleaning.

Consider preventive housekeeping, that is, reducing the decibel level of all those chores screaming at you to be done. Before I start listing preventive housekeeping measures, however, let's consider a more simplistic attitude to housework in general. Getting rid of guilt is even more important than getting rid of excess bric-a-brac (that's what this book is all about), and will do wonders for you. Here are a few generic tips.

- Take off your glasses so you can't see the dust.
- Don't try to do everything, especially not all at once.
- Try to enlist help – for love or money, preferably for love, but do not stoop to blackmail.
- Bow to the inevitable: to your own limitations; to circumstances beyond your control; to a husband who's a slob, children who hang their towels on the floor, a new baby who hasn't learned about sleeping through the night; to a day-after-day job and home tasks that pick up where the family doesn't. Today is not forever; it only feels like it.
- Simplify your household.
- Start by eliminating the unnecessary.
- Put small ornaments in a cabinet under glass so they won't need dusting.
- Buy big plants instead of smaller ones so that there are fewer of them to water.

- Take down your curtains. If you must have privacy try a large oriental fan in the window, or philodendron vines (remembering what I just said about plants), or vertical slat blinds (less dusting).
- Buy duvets for your beds.
- Get everyone in the house with the mentality of an eight-year-old to make his or her own bed. (My rule with my husband was always "last one out of bed makes it.")
- If you can't afford duvets then, as you have to replace your bed linen, color co-ordinate it for easy identification, sorting, and storing. You could consider not using color at all; one of the most organized persons I know buys white everything – towels, sheets, pillowcases, and so on (she puts her color elsewhere). Everything is thus interchangeable.
- Next time you're buying storage containers of any kind (for fridge, closet, wherever), buy ones with clear sides so you know what's inside without opening all of them.

All these things sound mindlessly simple, but so is housework. It's the cumulative effect that kills you.

- Duplicate things and save steps. Most families can't afford a vacuum cleaner on every floor but you can duplicate small cleaning aids where you need them: glass cleaner, cleanser, and paper towels in every bathroom; dusters or whiskbrooms where you want them; paper or plastic bags in every closet to clear out the debris in each room as you go along.
- Duplicate small tools on either side of your kitchen as well, so you're not always going back to the rack or drawer on the other side for the measuring cups or spoons, the wooden spoons, spatula, or tongs.
- Keep an extra, basic, tool kit in the kitchen (hammer, screwdriver, pliers) as well as in the basement work room.
- Keep cellulose tape everywhere and give the children their own, with strict rules about not removing Mother's Tape.

The idea, as Lillian Gilbreth first told us in her book on domestic management,[6] is to store everything at point of first use, so it comes to hand when you need it. Thus, (if you have the space) keep the ironing board up (you still iron?) and ready at all times, have several small mending baskets stationed around the house for fast fast fast repairs, and boxes of tissue everywhere – handy for coping with small spills, ashtrays (you still smoke?), reading glasses and noses.

You can duplicate other items as well. I keep reading glasses on my desk (designed specifically for use with my computer) and another pair in my purse. I always try to keep extra keys in handy places because I am terrified of losing keys. Manicure scissors are on a hook in the bathroom, in my make-up bag, and in my travel cosmetic case. On the other hand, Elaine St. James (*Simplify Your Life*) claims that when she had only one nail file she always knew where it was; when she bought several to scatter around, she could never find one. You know yourself better than St. James or I do.

Okay, more lists.

- Store stuff in the open: baskets look decorative on a kitchen wall, don't clutter up a cupboard, and are handy to use.
- Hang tools and utensils.
- Hang hats and toys and even bicycles (a good idea for an apartment-dweller).
- Find decorative grids and pegs to hang things on, and jewelry and mug trees for the counters. Things are not only handy when they're out in the open but somehow they manage to stay neater and cleaner.
- Find multi-uses for things and cut down on one-of-a-kind clutter.
- You know the idea of putting things in a box in the basement and if you don't need them for a year, give them away. That's things like shrimp de-shellers, oyster shuckers, meat larding needles, icing sugar sifters, chocolate graters, and gravy shakers. These are all products I have possessed and dispossessed over the years. (I kept my strawberry huller and my grandmother's nutmeg grater.) You'd be amazed how much you can do with one good knife.
- Find other resources than yourself to lean on and go ahead and lean. Children are very good at errands and it's good for them, teaches them about handling money, getting along with people, feeling

important. (Ditto husbands.) I used to hate it when my mother told me to phone for a dentist's appointment or arrange for something to be done, but it taught me how, at an early age. As soon as my daughters took cooking classes at school, I began the next summer to have them plan and cook a dinner at least one night a week. When it was time for my youngest (learning-disabled) son to learn how to cook, I bought him every "helper" and mix in sight and let him learn the basics from the very simple directions on the packages. I gained weight but he learned how to cook.

- Swap services with neighbors, not just barter on baby-sitting and carpools, but also on picking up something (not too heavy) while they're at an out-of-the-way, but favorite (cheese? pasta?) store, and do the same for them. Speaking of shopping,
- keep a master list and never go into a store without it. This saves money as well as time.

Superwomen are all very well, but don't think you're letting the side down if you're not one. Take it easy. Nowhere does this advice apply more clearly than in the area of your social life. Say no to invitations if you're really swamped; that way you don't have to pay anyone back. The energy you save may be your own. If you've been asked once too many times to bring along your famous antipasto or your fabulous rum cake, try saying "I can't," and don't explain.

As for paying back social debts, have one big open house and cover everyone in one fell bash. Or have a series of back-to-back dinners over several weekends and at least do all your desserts ahead. I know one woman who plans one dinner menu, cooks large amounts all at once and freezes them in party-sized portions. Then she gives a series of dinner parties and pays off all her debts. The only one who suffers is her husband who has to eat chicken tetrazzini four weeks running. Of course, you could decide not to have anyone over for dinner. That's the simplest of all.

This is not to say that you shortchange your friends, or deprive yourself of their company. Find other ways. Short notice, spur-of-the-moment invitations, when you feel like it, when you have the energy, the desire and the time, will never be spurned, not by real friends. And real friends are as happy with popcorn as with homemade pâté. It's you they want to see, not a gleaming house with flowers and candles and an exhausted hostess.

The biggest killer for busy people is the time (yours) that other people waste. You've probably seen the hostile letters people have written to their doctors or dentists charging them for the time they've spent in their waiting rooms. No one ever collects on these. But you don't have to let other people waste your time. Take a book with you, so that you don't have to read 1976 issues of "Sport & Field" or "Protein News." Or take a notebook (I never go anywhere without a notebook) and make a list while you're waiting. Plan your Christmas shopping or your next dinner party menu (see above). Last winter a friend of mine was stuck in an airport for four hours waiting for a plane to materialize. She pulled out a stationery notepad and wrote 20 letters while she waited, and caught up with all her correspondence. (Her brother was very surprised to hear from her!) Some people still knit, and that remains one of the most productive ways to spend other people's time. If you're in a lineup, as we are so frequently these days – in supermarkets, banks, drugstores, liquor stores or in front of movie houses, not to mention in the car at red lights and in heavy traffic – you can use that time, too, if you're an addicted knitter. But don't knit while you're driving. Learn to meditate. Once you get proficient at it, you can slip into a calmer state even while waiting forever in a queue. In short, set your own pace. The time and energy you save belong to you. Nerves too.

Christmas and Gift Giving

Speaking of nerves, Christmas is a nerve-making time of the year, with a score of 12 on the Holmes-Rahe Stress Scale. You can perform a lot of stress-reducing frugal tips and bring back some of the missing spirit at the same time if you rethink the whole jolly season.

Start with laughter. One of the funniest ways of saving money on gifts is the practice Jerry Seinfeld has called *re-gifting*. The episode which followed a gift as it made its way from recipient to recipient struck a chord in most viewers, and only seemed to leave reality when it wound up back in the hands of the original giver. But I know someone that happened to. A friend of mine received a distinctively labeled bottle of homemade wine, which he gave away. About a year later he received the exact same bottle from a totally different source.

I pass on items I can't use, as I'm sure most people do, but I'm careful not only about whom I give them to, but of the appropriateness of the gift. I keep a re-gifting drawer, much more useful than landfill.

Now take a good hard look at Buy Nothing Day (see p. 93), and decide whether you are capable of buying nothing. Before you do this you should rejig your gift list. I have seen any number of frugal recommendations to limit the amount of money spent on gifts, including for your own family. You could try setting an arbitrary limit per person and stick to it. The *GreenMoney Journal* reports that the Methodists came up with a "hundred-dollar holiday"; the limit on gifts per family is $100, with the emphasis on homemade gifts (home baking, jams and jellies, knitting and crafts) or invisible gifts (back rubs, baby-sitting, other services).

I know a large family that draws names. Each brother or sister gets one sibling to buy for, so that each one gets one good present. I also know a number of families now that use the Christmas Gift Voucher system. You don't give a gift without giving yourself with it. I've done this for a number of years when I visit my grandchildren, and not only with Christmas gifts.

I take a kit, either boxed or in a booklet, which has to be assembled and produced. It might be a store, or a house, or a space station; most frequently it is a theatre with plays or stories to act out. I help my little ones put it together and then we put on a show, sometimes even for an audience – their parents.

I know someone who gave her mentally challenged son a cookbook but didn't give herself with it, to help him read and choose and prepare recipes from it. I helped the boy, a friend of my son, taking him step-by-step through the preparation of a few dishes which he cooked, and writing down the directions in a simpler form so that he could make them again. I knew how to do all this because I had already done it with my son when he was first learning to cook. The gift of time and self is a precious one, one that can't be bought but that is worth more than diamonds. It saves money while it enriches a relationship.

Now how do we distinguish between saving time, saving money, saving energy, and saving the planet? And what about cutting corners and cutting waste? The question is, are you being good to yourself or to the planet? The answer is simple, if you're doing it right – both.

16

Barter and Community Currency

*There is a general lesson here that politicians from every country
should become acquainted with:
welfare programs can be replaced by imagination and creativity
if the right leadership is available.
Also, politicians get re-elected for providing such leadership.*
— Bernard A. Leitaer

Jack and the Beanstalk is the most famous story of barter I can think of. The beans Jack's mother planted inadvertently when she angrily tossed them out the window had been received in barter for a cow. There are other longer tales of barter, for example, the story of the slow-witted farmer who traded down a series of goods to end with nothing, and grateful for it. School kids, if we can believe the commercials, barter their lunches but will not trade anything for Lunchables®.

Barter is defined as "the exchange of one commodity or service for another without the use of money as a medium of exchange."[1] Nations and corporations and large as well as small struggling companies use barter to encourage trade, save money, promote products and curry favor. On a smaller scale, barter goes on between individual entrepreneurs and private citizens, often as a means of escaping taxes by not declaring income or reciprocal services. On the back fence level, any exchange of favors with a neighbor constitutes a kind of barter.

When I was a young married woman, having all those babies, my contemporaries and I performed a kind of barter. I remember for one of my little offspring, born conveniently four weeks before a friend's child, I bought a Jolly Jump-Up, one of those bouncy chairs that was supposed to strengthen a pre-toddler's legs (it would probably be condemned as unsafe now). Talk about planned obsolescence! The minute the kid was on her legs, the JJ-U was useless. I passed it on to my friend for two-thirds of the purchase price, as agreed. Four weeks later, she sold it to the third mother in the triumvirate for one-third of the retail price. After that, one of us was pregnant again (we did that in those days) and it started the rounds again, paid for.

We also traded sitting services, not, of course, when we were all seeing each other, but if one of the couples wanted to go to a movie on a weeknight, or if they both had separate meetings, I would go over and sit (leaving my husband to sit at home). Another week, our friends would return the compliment. No one counted hours or kept any accounting. It was straight trade, a favor for a favor.

My father was a young doctor, a general practitioner, in Manitoba, during the Depression. When I was born, Jack was considered to be both rich and rash, having a second child despite the disastrous economy. I guess it looked rich. We had a summer cottage on Lake Winnipeg; we had a live-in maid and a gardener and mother sent the laundry out; I went to a private school, driven home each day in a taxi; an artist sculpted a bust of me, which I still have, and my mother collected things. It was done with barter (and collection agencies).

The cottage on Lake Winnipeg was a wedding gift from my mother's parents, my Icelandic grandparents, who owned a general store (now a heritage building) in Gimli, Manitoba. The maid was more essential to my father than to my mother because the maid cooked for him and my aunt (his secretary) in the summer when mother was at the lake with my brother and me. She also answered the phone. The phone was a two-way lifeline and was never left untended in those days before voice mail.

The gardener was a handyman trying to pay off his son's appendectomy and his wife's latest confinement by doing odd jobs and watering my father's grass and liquor. The washing was done free of charge by a private laundry run by a convent orphanage-cum-detention home, my father's personal, private charity, inherited from his father. When there was an outbreak of measles among the orphans or when one of the delinquents had a baby, or when one of the nuns needed more treatment than prayer, my father used to come home and say he had done a big washing that day. I never met a washing machine until I was married.

I guess my father paid the tuition for my convent schooling, which he deemed essential in the days before public kindergarten, when I was already reading Grimm's fairy tales at age five but couldn't tell time. He may have had some initial help from his parents, who had hopes for me that his atheism might be countered by catechism. My father drove me to school in the morning; the cab at the end of the day was driven by another ex-patient in exchange for medical services rendered. A man tuned our piano regularly once a month, whether it needed it or not.

The sculptor was a woman who fooled around with modeling clay and whose husband was down on his luck. A bust of me, a Shirley Temple look-alike, was her finest work, left with its natural clay finish, untouched by her Kewpie-doll paints.

My father's deals began with straight barter, but got more complicated. When people couldn't pay their bills he tried to help them buy their groceries and pride. A professional man himself, somehow he always managed to hire totally untrained people to work for him. I had to ask for an extension for my M.A. thesis because the typist he engaged turned out to be a two-finger disaster unable to deal with footnotes. Jack also traded or, in a pinch, bought things.

"My, that's a handsome thingamajig," he'd say. "I don't suppose you'd be willing to part with it." That's how mother ended up with, among other things, seven family Bibles, 12 paperweights, 18 hat pins, and 65 cookie jars, all purchased by my father. By contrast, very few people paid him.

Medical treatment isn't like furniture: you can't reclaim it. Once the flu is over, the dislocated shoulder relocated, the tonsils removed, the baby born, why pay the doctor? Out of pain, out of mind. Shelter, food, clothes and entertainment take priority over illnesses past. Collection agencies couldn't reclaim goods but they could hound and badger and threaten until attention and money were paid. For their efforts, they took 50 percent of the money. Still, my father would shrug, 50 percent of something is better than 100 percent of nothing.

Then Workmen's Compensation was invented, and medical tests (for insurance), and Manitoba Medical Service (MMS), and with them the reports and records and documents and case histories and forms and questionnaires and bills and receipts and statements and verification – all the paper work we love to hate.

"How do you know this is the patient's urine sample?" one questionnaire probed.

"Watched him like a hawk," my father wrote.

But there was money, real cash not cookie jars at the end of the line.

That was my first lesson in depression economics – in barter. Barter tends to surface strongly as the economy dips. Swapping thrives in a recession, or in a closed society, like Hornby Island. In this tiny island in the Gulf Islands there is a Free Store where the inhabitants take all their unwanted goods for others to choose and use and where they can "buy" other people's stuff that appeals to them. I admired a clock in a friend's house on Hornby and she said proudly, "I bought it at the Free Store." Generic barter at its best, no strings. No wrapping either. You might be the one to start a Free Store in your area, not only helping yourself and your neighbors to bargains but also doing your bit to keep stuff out of landfill. Such a swap shop works better in a closed society like an island so that you are not running in direct, resented competition with the local garage and yard sales.

Some dumpsites now have stalls where you can buy used, still-usable goods for peanuts. Thanks to the efficiency of planned obsolescence it is possible to equip a home with others' castoffs. This is not quite barter because sometimes cash is involved, but trades can be negotiated as well.

Barter starts with a simple quid pro quo: you scratch my back, I'll scratch yours. But then one day your scratching buddy's back isn't itchy. She wants someone to wash her windows. Your arms aren't up to that. So you owe her one. You suggest you keep a record of this debt, but she suggests you could bake that fabulous cake of yours for her husband's birthday. And she'd like to make a certificate of merit for him but she needs someone who's good at calligraphy. Someone else who is an ace at windows but who doesn't want a back rub either, but who did windows for a calligrapher suggests you all trade around. By this time you need to write it down, and keep a record of people's skills and what they owe or have earned, especially when the lady with the pen decides to redecorate her living room and wants to know if she can get a deal on paint. Now you're into goods as well as services and you have to figure out how to price them as well as keep track of them. And not only you. The Income Tax Department is very interested in any kind of barter/exchange that works like income and is therefore taxable. Once there's a paper trail, it can be tracked. Enter community currencies.

Community Currencies

The shift from money to electronics is as important
as the earlier shift from barter to money.
– John Naisbitt

During World War II, cigarettes were the barter item of choice on the black market. They became a currency, with values according to quantity. I think it had something to do with Supply and Demand. I took one economics course in high school and learned two phrases; that was one of them. The other was Law of Diminishing Returns. Since then I've added one more law – Gresham's. Armed with those, how am I going to explain community currencies in a book about the simple life? Economics are beyond me, but human nature is not. Let's talk about pogs.

Pog was the name given to a milk bottle top that kids started collecting to play with, making up a game that's kind of a cross between croquinole and marbles. Some entrepreneur spotted the trend and began to manufacture pogs, really neat ones, with pictures (ads, depending on the maker; you can imagine what's on Disney pogs), different weights, strengths and scarcity and, therefore, value. I interviewed an 11-year-old capitalist who was cornering the pog market in Barrie, Ontario, when I met her. Assisted by her parents who floated her a loan to buy stock and rent tables at local flea markets to trade and sell her growing and admirable stock, she took on an assistant and diversified, adding pog display albums and special containers to hold prize pogs. She was so busy with her buying, selling and trading, keeping her books, recording her profits and loan payments that she stopped playing pogs. At least pogs don't rust, like some treasures. They do, however, go out of style. This happens to money, too.

Land used to be the mark of wealth, or at least of security – land and cattle. In fact, of course, the word *capital* comes from the same root as cattle, cap or head. We still sometimes speak of people having a thousand head, well, Texans or Masai say that, maybe. Both *cattle* and land are still indicators of wealth, but they are less portable than some kind of uniform object made of metal or paper which has been agreed upon to represent an ability to pay for goods or services. "Legal tender," it's called on Canadian money, meaning that it's legal to proffer it in payment. American bills are identified as a "Federal Reserve Note," sort of like an IOU, which the government will honor at whatever the going rate of honoring is. This seems to be a fluctuating, arbitrary evaluation, depending on other influencing factors of the general economy. Whatever, coins and paper notes were invented because they were portable, a more easily distributed method of exchange than, say, whale's teeth, sugar, salt, gold or cigarettes – all forms of currency at one time or another. It used to be that the paper and metal forms of legal tender were easier to carry around than those other things, but sometimes they weren't. I remember reading that in Germany before the war (WWII), people had to carry their money in wheelbarrows in order to go and buy bread. That's called inflation and I won't go into that here. Anyway, money, as such, is becoming irrelevant now, for different reasons.

In civilized – no, industrialized – countries we use other means than cash for paying for what we buy: checks, credit cards, charge accounts, all of which are really just various forms of formal, documented IOUs. Ready cash is getting scarce, especially small coins. In Canada we have loonies and toonies which still have a little buying power: coffee, a newspaper, a muffin. Most check-out counters in small, cash-and-carry stores now have a dish or a box for pennies and nickels for people who are short of or who don't want to carry the small stuff. We used to need small coins for phone booths and parking meters. Now the phone companies are issuing digital cards worth x amount of our own money, wherever it is, in return for x number of minutes. Meters will not be far behind, I'm sure. As for highway tolls, soon cars will be charged electronically and no one will ever have the chance to perfect a left-hand, backhand toss of coins into a collection basket. Money, real money, countable and usable, is becoming obsolete. It's a wonder street beggars get any change at all.

Theoretically, every coin or piece of paper we tender as payment is based on something, a standard of value which the currency represents. It used to be gold until the world went off the gold standard in the 1920s and then off the gold bullion standard in 1931.[2] After World War II, international trade was carried on according to the gold-exchange standard, rather than to any fluctuating currencies. Actually, most nations fixed their currencies to the US dollar and maintained dollar reserves in the United States; this was known as the "key currency" country.

At the Bretton Woods International Conference in 1944, the International Monetary Fund was created and given the responsibility of maintaining stable exchange rates around the world.

Then in 1968, after confidence in the US dollar had weakened, leading to a run on US gold reserves, a "two-tier system" was created. In the official tier, comprised of central bank gold traders, the value of gold was set at $35 an ounce and payments of gold to non-central bankers was prohibited. In the free-market tier – all the nongovernmental gold traders – the price of gold was set by supply and demand, with gold and the US dollar recognized as the major reserve assets for the world's central banks. By 1971 the drain on US gold reserves was so great that the United States abandoned gold convertibility, leaving the world without a single, unified international monetary system. Nothing material actually backs the currencies of the world.

In essence now, gold is obsolete. Where does that leave money? I'm convinced it's all make-believe. We do two things with money. One, we assign a standard of measure to things, in terms of comparative value; two, we agree to accept money as the most efficient medium of exchange, except when we run out of it. Then we have to figure out how the exchange differs, depending on which country's currency is the strongest on the international market. By the end of this century when the new European Currency Unit (ECU) has replaced the different national currencies, it is expected that it will be the second (after the US dollar) most commonly used currency in the international bond market. It reminds me of that condescending egg explaining things to Alice:[3]

"When I use a word," Humpty Dumpty said, in rather a scornful tone, "it means just what I choose it to mean – neither more nor less."

"The question is," said Alice, "whether you can make words mean so many different things."

"The question is," said Humpty Dumpty, "which is to be master – that's all." He might just as well have been talking about money.

It hurts my brain to think about it. It's all in our heads, anyway, completely arbitrary, as we all agree to agree about what money means, whether or not it makes any dollars and sense to us. The mind-boggling billions that are traded on world markets have nothing to do with our daily bread and the dismaying price of a seven-grain loaf, or do they? Money becomes important when it stops being there, when it escalates not only out of mind but out of pocket and sight, too.

The possibly apocryphal story goes that the grandson of American mathematician Dr. Edward Kasner (1878-1955) made up the word for the biggest number anyone could think of. Googol is a silly sound and the amount is silly, too, incomprehensible, in fact – a one followed by a hundred zeros. No one was ever going to handle a number that big, so it seemed like a good idea to use the silly word. I'm not too sure about googol anymore.

When I was growing up, million was a rare number. You could go bankrupt in Monopoly owing $2,500 to the owner of Boardwalk and Park Place. Now corporations are merging or going down to defeat (only to surface again, more resilient than a phoenix, rising from the ashes of their burning ambition) with billions of dollars going with them. Well, not with them, exactly, but out. For a while. And with them go jobs and people.

Human beings tend to stay down and out longer than corporations, which is why some people need a new currency, something they can understand and use to buy new shoes and bread, something they can – I was going to say "bank on," but what they require is not bankable cash but usable notes to exchange for something they need. Complexity is very hard to simplify, but these days everyone is trying to do it, especially when it comes to money. You should be grateful I had only that one high school course in economics. Are you ready for Gresham's Law?

Sir Thomas Gresham (1519–1579), an English merchant and founder of The Royal Exchange in London, was mistakenly given credit in the 19th century for Gresham's Law, which dates back to the 16th century: Bad money drives out good.

The *Encyclopaedia Brittanica* explains the law simply: "If two coins have the same nominal value but are made from metals of unequal value, the cheaper will tend to drive the other out of circulation." Even today, that's why silver dollars never get spent but go out of circulation into someone's coin collection or piggy bank. Loonies lord it over them. Thus, it follows that I may never get my hands on any sizeable amount of legal tender. Maybe I should issue my own scrip. This is what community currencies are doing, although some aren't using scrip.

Local currency based on an exchange of goods and services is not a new idea, in fact, it's centuries old. Ignoring other centuries, I can tell you that in the early 1930s a town called Woergl, in the Austrian Alps, suffering like the rest of the world from the Great Depression, issued its own currency, a kind of scrip they pretended was money, and it worked, drawing world-wide attention. The people of Woergl simply traded their labor and material rather than money, keeping track of their debits and credits with scrip, and caused the (local) depression to end. In the United States, the Confederate Rebels issued their own money when the North declared war and they formed a separate Congress – that's not a good example. After the Riel Rebellion in 1869 the Canadian government issued scrip to the Métis. Each piece of "scrip money" was worth 240 acres of land or $240. Needing food, most of the people took cash rather than land. Bad move.

In the 1970s, Ralph Borsodi and Robert Swann launched the Constant, in Exeter, New Hampshire. It was a kind of money based on a value system using 30 different commodities in a stock index similar to the Dow Jones average. It was called Constant because its creators expected it would be more reliable than the national currency. It circulated for a year, proving a point and gaining national publicity. One reporter asked if such a currency was legal and Borsodi, who was an economist, advised him to ask the Treasury Department. This was the answer: "We don't care if he issues pine cones, as long as it is exchangeable for dollars so that transactions can be recorded for tax purposes."[4]

Ay, there's the rub. No matter what medium of exchange you trade in, if you're ahead of the game you're behind the eight ball, tax-wise.

Remember E. F. Schumacher (*Small is Beautiful*)? In 1982, Great Barrington, home of the E. F. Schumacher Society, began an operation leading to a Berkshire currency. A nonprofit organization called SHARE (Self-Help Association for a Regional Economy) was incorporated with the intent of establishing an organizational base for a local currency. SHARE's first moves were by way of making productive loans to local small entrepreneurs offering quality goods and services for local consumption; people unable to get the banks even to consider a loan for them, or if they did, with prohibitively high interest rates. SHARE members signed on and opened savings accounts in a designated bank. These accounts were used as collateral to guarantee the loans; essentially, people were underwriting themselves. It worked. SHARE loans, still going, still productive, are not consumer-oriented but designed to cover only equipment or inventory. A newsletter keeps members informed as to what their money is doing.

The project has expanded since then, with variations, including one member, the owner of a deli in Great Barrington, who followed SHARE's suggestion that he issue his own Deli Dollars as a self-financing method, which led to an experiment in Berk-Shares, a forerunner of Ithaca's Hours.

In the summer of 1991, Ithaca businessman Paul Glover heard a radio interview with someone from the Schumacher Society staff describing Deli Dollars and Berk-Shares, and that inspired him to launch another local currency. (Actually, he had tried a few years earlier, with LETSystem, but things didn't work out.) Ithaca, New York, is now considered the leader in the current trend to an alternative currency system,[5] known as Ithaca Hours. Described in the May/June 1997 *Utne Reader* as one of the ten most enlightened towns in America (Toronto, Canada, brought the number to 11), this college town of 30,000 people has its own bank notes, Ithaca Hours, imprinted with "In Ithaca We Trust." Quoted on their Home Page, the people behind the plan for this local currency say that "while dollars make us increasingly dependent on multinational corporations and bankers, Hours reinforce community trading and expand commerce which is more accountable with our concern for ecology and social justice." If it sounds like a plug, it should. Glover, the founder of Ithaca Hours, has seen the strength of this local currency grow to the point where the bills are accepted as readily as American dollars in about 350 local businesses. Some $60,000 in Hours have been issued in the last five and a half years and traded by about 2,000 people, generating an estimated $2 million worth of business. The above-mentioned Ithaca Home Page, updated in June 1997, lists 43 "Hour Cities" up and running, including five in Canada, with 34 planning to or about to launch, including another four in Canada.

The Hours system is not the quid pro quo of straight time-barter: my time for your time. Ithaca Hours are negotiable like cash and can be used to buy food or any goods or services offered by participating businesses – and not just weird ones that wouldn't sell anything otherwise. Some workers are willing to take part of their pay in Hours and people don't mind receiving change in Hours bills, which come in four denominations: the 1/4-hour note, the 1/2-, the 1-, and the 2-hour notes, valid within a 20-mile radius of downtown Ithaca. The top value is $10, the average hourly wage in that region. The point of the whole operation is to circulate business among the local commercial enterprises and to keep money in the community. A city-wide system that keeps money in the community and gives buying power to people, especially those who might not otherwise be able to buy anything, can't be all bad. It may be an idea whose time has come. The concept of money as we know it now is only about 4,000 years old. Maybe it has passed its prime, if you'll pardon the pun. Who knows what the future may hold?

Michael Linton in Canada is convinced the future will hold LETSystems, a more sophisticated and transformative corollary of Ithaca Hours which, while they were easier to start, will prove, he is sure, "extremely difficult to keep on the road." Linton, a business consultant, was born in Britain and emigrated to the west coast of Canada in the 1970s. He is credited with masterminding this whole current trend away from what we remember calling money and leading it toward community currency, a virtual means of holding a community (usually urban) together.

In the early 1980s, he launched Landsman Community Services Ltd. as a Canadian company designed to promulgate the LETSystem on a global scale. Begun in 1983 in the Comox Valley on Vancouver Island, the system has spread to over 800 communities in the world,[6] and was set (at time of writing) for a major launch in Vancouver in the fall of 1997, to be followed in Toronto.

Backed by the Citizen's Bank, a socially conscious, virtual bank (no branches) owned by the city of Vancouver, the system doesn't use an alternate form of currency (scrip/Hours). It just adds "a wheel to your bike," as Linton puts it. He says another currency would only be confusing. I think if there ever were any LETS dollars printed, Linton would beat out George Washington or a grain elevator any day as the icon of choice. LETS, by the way, is an acronym with differing translations. It might stand for Local Exchange Trading System or it might also be Local Employment Trading System. Linton prefers the acronym to stand for itself, as in LETS do it!

I requested an interview with Michael Linton before I knew all this, having come across his name in an article in *Chatelaine* magazine ("Swap till you drop," August 1997) and then in an E-mail from my friend, Canadian novelist Joy Kogawa, who gave me a reference so he'd be willing to talk to me. I offered to phone him direct or have him call me collect but he graciously assumed the cost of a call. Unemployed for the last few years because he is spending all his time on this alternate money system, Linton manages to pay his phone bills and eat because his wife, bless her, is still working and supporting him. Presumably this will all change soon when he is reimbursed for his time, efforts and expertise. In the meantime, he is a man with a mission.

As American futurist Hazel Henderson says, "the key to the success of a community currency is trust," and LETS is proving trustworthy. It works on two basic requirements: a record of services "bought" or "sold" and a directory of services available, both easy to track with a computer and the Internet. A value system still applies and so does exchange, but the nature of money, as we know it, may change forever. Here's how LETS works.

Remember my baby-sitting analogy, and how one good turn deserved another? That's it, except a computer keeps track of it and every deal is calculated partly on money (the legal tender we all know) and partly on credit for services rendered. I charge you $25 for baby-sitting: $10 in cash and $15 in credits which goes into my account, while yours is debited by $15. Now I can spend my virtual $15, plus legal tender, to get something I want. You can buy something, too, because you are allowed to run a negative balance. What you owe encourages others to draw on your services so that you can work off your debt.

The question arises, what if someone skips town leaving a negative balance? Virtually nothing. They can't take it with them, and the economy has already been stimulated. It doesn't seem to have been a problem; the honor system holds. Participants can watch each other's balance and encourage fair use. All the trading details are available to anyone holding an account within the system, so it's pretty hard to hide. If you don't like someone's debt load, you can suggest he work it off before you deal with him. No interest is charged or paid on accounts. All transactions, of course, are subject to income tax[7] as well as GST and PST (where applicable).

Use one computer, use them all: the Internet offers LETSystems the opportunity to go global. LETS lays down a safe paper trail – well, not paper, exactly, but safe – because encryption makes it possible to exchange national currencies as easily as local currencies. Encryption-based digital signature technology makes my head hurt, too. It's voluntary complexity. However, I am simple enough to put my trust in people's promises, so maybe it will be okay. Users say LETS is "just like barter" or "better than barter," but I think it's much more flexible. I like the idea that it is a social movement rather than a mere economic system.

So how does such a complex system affect us in our attempt to find simplicity? All we want to do is slow down a little, ease up a little, make a little sense of our lives, maybe raise our eyes toward the horizon or heaven, a little. Do we have to have a whole new economic system to do this? Maybe we do if we don't have much of the old-style legal tender to get along with. It's getting more and more complicated to simplify our lives. Maybe this LETSystems will help.

PART V

Living More Simply

Teach us to delight in simple things
And mirth that has no bitter springs;
Forgiveness free of evil done,
And love to all men 'neath the sun.

– Rudyard Kipling

17

Getting Organized

One of these years, I've got to get organized.

That was the line on a paperweight I once owned, showing a nebbish lying on a couch with piles of stuff around him, worrying, but not doing anything about it. How is it possible, we wonder, when we know what we have to do, not to do it? How can we sit/lie here and do nothing? How can we be totally sincere about wanting to simplify our lives and yet walk around in such a complicated mess? How can we live in such clutter? Easy. We're human. It's one of the most characteristic behavior patterns of human beings, this pushmepullyou approach to life. We say one thing and do another, like vow that we want to lose weight and exercise while we continue to eat and be a couch potato; like declare we don't believe a word commercials tell us and keep on buying what they advertise; like claim to be downscaling, practicing thrift at every flea market, and coming home with a new digital player with sound that has to be heard to be believed; like profess a sincere desire to live simply and keep on wallowing in squalid complexity. Because we're human.

It's not merely a case of getting organized, although that's a big part of it. If that were all! By this time everyone knows all about Alan Lakein and Shirley Conran, Efficiency Expert and Superwoman, respectively, and others like them who for outrageous sums per hour will come and impose order on your life, or sell you their books. They have all sorts of cute little slogans and directives, some more realistic (for me) than others. Here's a popular one: Handle each piece of paper only once. I can't do that. Elaine St. James (*Simplify Your Life*) modifies paper to piece of mail, but that's almost as hard. She also changes (slightly) another tried-and-true method of "uncluttering." Using "Dave's system," she tells you to put all the things you no longer use but can't bear to throw out into a box or boxes labeled with only a date some two or three years hence, but without a list of contents. Look at the labels once a year but don't peek inside. When the expiry date has passed, throw out the box without opening it. This, of course, does terrrible things to landfill.

I first heard that advice applied to kitchen utensils. It's not a bad idea, except for things like specially made wedding cake tins which you saved for your daughter's wedding 30 years later, or a silver champagne bucket for ditto. I solved this problem once Kate's wedding was over by passing these items on to her. After she was married (wearing a dress designed for her, that she will have to cope with), I sold my wedding dress for $50 to a Vintage Shop. I still have my handmade silver kid wedding shoes. Don't ask.

The stuff-in-a-box idea works on other things as well. I used to put the family mending in a box and when it no longer fit anyone I knew, I gave it away. I hate sewing even more than I hate clutter. If I lose a button on a blouse, the blouse goes out. I learned this the hard way, keeping an impaired garment until it was out of style and still buttonless. I'm sure everyone has simple tricks like this.

In your zeal for cleaning out the cupboards, one large area of your life stumps you. You are terrified to throw out important papers. You think that some things simply can't be simplified, like files. Most people have a fear of filing and an even worse terror of unfiling. Most people hang on to paper too long, afraid they'll need it as soon as they toss it. They're right, they usually do. It's fears like this that make most people let the paper proliferate and the files pile. They just buy more filing cabinets or shoe boxes as necessary to take care of the mess. Income tax receipts, records and returns are bad enough; GST makes every piece of paper a clutterer's nightmare. Experts call this attitude hoarder's syndrome, but there's no pleasure in it. Who wants to be a paper miser?

Experts, as I say, make big money organizing other people's papers. You could do it for yourself, if you only knew for sure what was safe to toss. You have to know yourself pretty well, to know what you're comfortable with paring down, and you have to decide what isn't going to be worth a fortune to your grandchildren, or of some vital interest to a social historian. You never know what posterity might prize, so you don't want to take any chances. However, if you're serious in your desire to clear a path to your desk, there are some basic guidelines you can follow.

For tax documents most of you are safe keeping them for five years, untouched. Up to five years, the treasurer general may want to have a look at them. After that, you could probably toss the receipts and keep only the copies of your returns. They make nice mementoes of the years that were, and don't take up too much space. If you have a complicated life, with sundry investments, big capital gains, or (like me) a bizarre self-employment record, you might like to keep your records longer, say up to seven years, in case the government wants to take a look. I was actually audited once; my examiner concluded I was painfully honest but rather stupid. Even if you don't make enough income to be taxable, like a poor student (see students, p. 132) or an astute investor living off her nontaxable dividends, it's a good idea to file a return anyway.

Some papers should never be burned, like your paid-up mortgage. I've seen movies and read stories where people burn their mortgage to celebrate when they've paid it off, but it's not a good idea. You still need the proof that piece of paper provides. I used mine recently to assure my bank that I was a good risk for a line of credit. You also need to keep the complete records of your RRSPs, RESPs (see pp. 119, 130) and other investments. In the latter case, your annual statements will give you the rundown for the year so you can discard the quarterly reports. Keep these files until you sell the investment, and then hang on for another five or six years, just to be safe.

Regarding your home, keep relevant records and receipts for all the work done on it: painting, renovations, repairs and so on. I recently checked a painting contract because I couldn't remember the brand and color of the paint on the house and I needed to buy more for some touch-up work. Your receipts for utilities and other related records are useful, too, to give you a clear idea of your maintenance costs. If you go to sell the house, you can show them to a prospective buyer to give some idea of the expenses. Keep your GST receipts for the requisite five or six years, too. So far I've scarcely emptied a file, have I?

In this case, it's not the tossing, it's the organizing you need. You knew that. I am not about to tell you how to set up a filing system. If you know the alphabet, you don't need me. For years before I could afford a steel filing cabinet, I used cardboard cartons that exactly fit the dimensions of a file folder. Now you can buy fairly inexpensive pieces of furniture which double as endtables or support a slab to make a desk but which are fitted with hanging files. Get some.

I actually wrote a booklet called *The Shoebox Guide*, replacing my earlier booklet, *Where Is Everything?* The organization that commissioned these books has cancelled publication so you can't get one for free anymore. You used to be able to get a poor (because less detailed) imitation from some financial institutions, not as thorough as mine. However, they've probably cut their expenses too and figure you can fill your own shoe box.

I know one woman who took my list of things you need after your husband dies,[1] collected all the stuff, and put it in a small steel safe under her bed. Her husband was a bit dismayed when he found out what it was for, but she said she felt much more serene.

Calendars are good. I love calendars, appointment books, week-at-a-glances (weeks-at-a-glance), monthly planners, almost any kind of paper with boxes or grids that I can fill in and feel as if I'm budgeting my time effectively in order to create quality time. Everybody wants quality time, quantities of it. Bulletin boards are nice, too. Every office should have several: one for appointments, one for reminders, one for snappy sayings, one for little bits of paper you'll lose if you don't thumbtack them somewhere, but no photographs. Pictures, kids' artwork and recipes are for the fridge door. The outside of a fridge is almost as important as the inside these days, maybe more so. Whoever invented fridge magnets deserves the royalties. Also Post-it® notes. (I heard they were a mistake that paid off.) I am not digressing. You need lots of things to help you get organized. Also lists, new ones every day.

Always seed your list with things you've already done so you can tick them off and feel as if you've accomplished something. Plan more than you can possibly do because when you don't do it all you can reassure yourself that your plan was unrealistic in the first place and feel better.

Invent acronyms or initials for some of the things that have to go on each day's list, like BDT. That's what I used to write in my other life (when I was a housewife); BDT stood for BED, DUST, TIDY. It took me quite a while to learn my way around those imperatives. I persuaded my husband and my kids to make their beds; I took off my glasses so I couldn't see the dust; I put things in baskets and neat piles so at least they weren't scattered. That saved a lot of time and energy.

I'll tell you what squander more energy and usurp more space than they deserve: wasteful emotions. Envy, vengefulness, competitiveness, anger (even irritation, though I always give it a little head room), and – worst of all – pride; these are the real sources of clutter. Grudges fill up a horrible amount of space and leave you less storage room for pleasant memories. You want to clear your shelves and make room for things like forgiveness, tolerance, humility, generosity and compassion. And while you're at it, be sure to find space for slow fuses.

18

Satisfaction, as in I Can't Get No

The greatest wealth is to live content with little,
for there is never want where the mind is satisfied.
– Lucretius

A half a century ago (longer!) when I was first given an allowance and a lecture on the importance of saving money, I took it to heart. I dropped my entire 50 cents into an inaccessible bank, the kind of thick-headed little pig that had to be broken to open it. Oops. Too late, I realized I had no money to cover my modest but necessary expenses. No Saturday movie (costing a dime then), no penny candy, no church collection. Fortunately, my father noticed what I had done and floated me a loan. Thus, early in life did I learn about savings, debt and deficit spending, and also about the consequences of impulsive behavior.

That's what a lot of people are doing now when they decide to simplify their lives, making drastic decisions they won't be able to live with, let alone enjoy, moving first and thinking later. They follow a scorched earth policy and realize too late that they still need to live on the earth they scorched. They cut back too much, too soon, without assessing their bottom-line needs and their own quirky preferences. People who retire, especially those who take early retirement, blithely burn their library cards and move to other parts of the country, not as frequently out of Canada as formerly because of mounting out-of-country health care costs, but often to milder climates far away from where they have worked and lived, without even a decent trial run. This kind of simplification often causes more complications than meet the eye charts. I mean, do they give a thought to their medical and dental records, and finding new professionals to help them?

I've seen other high-minded, fuzzy-thinking people move to lake country like mine, equipping their part-time rural (never rustic) homes with all the appliances, including dishwashers and air-conditioners, powerful inboard motors, sea- and ski-doos and only then becoming rabid conservationists as they worry about zebra mussels and higher taxes without a thought for their aging septic tanks and the water table or for the families who go to the local schools and need the area hospitals.

I've been meeting and talking with older people like myself who also don't need schools, for obvious reasons, but who do need hospitals. The happiest ones are those who have made small changes, not always transforming their lifestyles but adjusting them. One single woman took her drastic change by degrees, moving from England to Toronto while still quite young in order to be closer to her sister, and then changing jobs and moving to a small town in the lake country where she plans to stay in her little house for the rest of her life. She had a summer cottage next door to her sister's family but when they sold theirs, she sold hers, and gave the money to her nieces and nephews, preferring that they use it while she's alive and not wanting to pay interest on money she says she doesn't need.

Another single woman, twice married and once widowed, sold her large house and moved to a much smaller one in a nearby, smaller town, investing the money she made on the sale to support herself. Another younger woman, after two failed marriages, bought her own little house in the city and rents the basement apartment to pay the mortgage.

A couple on the West Coast took a (forced) early retirement and winterized the wife's family cottage in a small resort town on the Strait of Georgia. I told them if or when their pension incomes cease to meet rising costs, they have a perfect setup for a B and B. I personally know half a dozen people in places like Stratford and Niagara-on-the-Lake, Ontario, who are happily catering to bed-and-breakfast customers during the season. They just had to buy more sheets and learn how to bake delicious muffins from a secret recipe (mix).

I had briefly as a client (in a writing seminar) a man who left a business job in the city for a small cabin on a lake and who does odd-job carpentry to support himself while he writes, still unpublished but happy.

Another client, a married woman whose husband was retiring, decided to move to their (winterized) summer home and write, leaving her astonished spouse free to golf in Florida and come and visit at Thanksgiving and Christmas. That's really downsizing!

Some years ago before this current trend, I saw friends, a married couple with four children, sell their house, store their treasures, and take their kids across Europe in a camper van for a year. That wasn't all that simple, but it was educational.

My first strip-trip was an investigation, for which I was paid, but the value of my discoveries far outweighed the fee. Twenty years ago I left my Toronto apartment and went to live in a rooming house in the east end of the city for three weeks. I did it on my own suggestion as an assignment for the *Toronto Star*, proposing to see what living was like on the other side of retirement. I took the amount of money then available from the Old Age Pension, plus the Guaranteed Income Supplement, and found myself a room in a house with a smoke detector in the upper hall and a landlady on the premises, two necessities, I was told, to protect me from (a) fire, and (b) rape by other residents. At that time, two-thirds of women over 65 were living below the poverty line, their sole income being the OAP and GIS; that figure is down to 40 percent now, not because government assistance has increased so much but because some women have worked outside the home and are getting CPP (Canada Pension Plan) money, or have managed to invest a bit for some modest investment income.

Anyway, there I was experiencing my first (drastically) simplified lifestyle. I took with me a pair of sheets, a blanket and a pillow, and a small bathroom mat to keep my feet from freezing on the cold floor when I got out of bed in the morning. My room was furnished with a single bed, a small wooden table and straight chair, a cupboard for clothes, a shelf for a pot and a few dishes and glasses, to which equipment I added a stock pot. A small two-burner stove, with an oven that worked if the burners didn't, offered two heats: on and off. I shared a bathroom and a fridge down the hall with the other (male) boarders.

I learned where to shop for day-old bread and found an Elderly Persons Centre that kept store on Thursday afternoons when I could buy potatoes and carrots by the one and talk to other old-age pensioners. I picked up free, used newspapers on streetcars, which I seldom rode because it was cheaper to walk; from the trash; or in the local library, where I was allowed to read on site. Library hours have been cut since then; I wonder where old people are going now, to read and keep warm. My editor had told me to buy a winter coat while I was living in this other country, and to have guests for a couple of meals. Both projects presented a challenge and took me a lot of time, comparison shopping for the coat, turning a cheap fowl into chicken crêpes for my guests.

I have described this adventure in other books (my cookbook and my writing book, among others) but it's interesting in this context because of what I learned about my own lifestyle and because of the remarkable temptation I encountered. This dress rehearsal made me aware of what I missed and what I would be wise to hang on to when the time came for the real thing.

One is a private bathroom. I used so much Pine-Sol and air freshener in the communal bathroom that one of my fellow roomers, courting me, presented me with pine-scented incense because he had noticed the "perfume" I was using and thought I must love pine. In a study on Women and Ageing, conducted by the Advisory Council on the Status of Women, it was found that more single old women than old men manage to have a private bathroom, no matter what their circumstances. I can understand that. Men splash.

Two is a phone. I had to check on my mother every week and it was cold standing in a phone booth feeding quarters into the phone to pay for a call to Winnipeg.

Three is wine. I did finally buy some cheap sherry, not a good move. While the act of pouring and raising a libation helped the ambience, the taste left a lot to be desired.

I have not previously described in print the total, unexpected surprise this exploration revealed to me. I was so disturbed by it that I actually sought some counseling to help me understand it. At that time, three of my children were almost independent but not fully. Liz was in Montreal in graduate school; Kate was just home from a year in Europe and Israel, living at home until she got a stake and a job; John was at Guelph University, an undergraduate, still living at home during the summer while he worked to pay his tuition. Matt, my brain-damaged son, was still at home with a huge ordeal ahead of him that fortunately neither of us then anticipated. My widowed mother was in Winnipeg and I remember standing there at that cold pay phone inviting her east to live down the hall from me (in a studio apartment) so I could look after her. I was alone, that is, widowed, trying to make a living, and still more or less responsible for all these people.

So here was my temptation: to disappear. It occurred to me how nice it would be to wipe away my past and sink into the city without a trace. I could live out my life in an anonymous room while I read my way through the Toronto Public Library.

My counselor called it The Temptation of the Hermit, but it was more than a hermitic life I craved. I wanted not only to be alone but to be free, to be clear of all encumbrances and liens on me, to be able to do what I wanted, when I wanted, and not to be responsible for other people. I didn't need much money, didn't want things. I just wanted to be left alone. I hated the thought of going back, of being so endlessly, heavily busy looking after my loved ones. It wasn't a desire for the simple life that I had, it was a wish for no life at all. I wouldn't have lasted a month, of course, if I had split. I am by nature a nurturer. As long as there's someone around who needs my nurturance, I'm there. Actually, I'm there whether anyone needs it or not, which is one of the reasons I live where I do so I will not be lured into nurturing instead of writing.

This is not a character analysis of your guide and mentor here. This is a valuable lesson to be learned from someone who tried an early run at the simple life – drastically simple! – and came back wiser and more prepared. When you finally do go simple, make sure you choose the right formula for you.

It's hard to cut back without having a very clear idea of how to go about it. It's hopeless to try without having a firm conviction that it's necessary, and that it's a good thing to do. Very few people can live on principles alone. Principles are all very well for New Year's Resolutions and year-end accounting, but daily acts are going to be a lot easier if they make sense, if they're fairly easy, if some reasonable satisfaction is gained from them. Sweeping changes begin with small strokes. They're like diets: people have to see some immediate results and feel good about what they're doing. And not be too hungry.

We all have a drive to consume something, one way or another, and it's a good thing. As I keep saying, our consumer habits are what make the economy go round so we have to be careful not to upset the apple cart. We have to keep eating apples so they won't spoil and leave the vendor with unsold, rotten apples. If we all decided to drop out tomorrow and quit spending, the results would be catastrophic.

I've already discussed the careful training we've all received as efficient, inexorable consumers. Our needs and wants, scarcely distinguishable, have been analyzed and catered to with increasing skill (and cynicism) over the decades. We think we know when we're being manipulated and sold a bill of goods but we have no idea how completely. Over and over again we push caution away as we plunge into debt, wreck the environment, and find ourselves surrounded by things. One seemingly good thing seems to lead to another as we go for matched sets, newer models, improved designs. This, as I say, is what makes the economy go round. What would the GNP do without us? In God we trust, the god of mammon, and we spread it around. There are many metaphors for money; it has been rightly called manure because it makes things grow when it's spread around. When we stop spending, things stop growing and a recession begins, or worse, a depression. So what would happen if we all stopped spending at once? We might start a war.

If and as we change our spending habits we are going to have to consider the effects on business and people. There is a difference, of course, between what we spend and what we consume. It may just be that we will continue to move away from consumption of goods as we move more and more into the purchase of services. The late American money expert, Sylvia Porter, predicted that people would be buying services rather than goods. That's mainly because no one does anything for anyone anymore for free. What mothers and neighbors and friends and fathers used to do out of love and good will are deeds that must be paid for now. We cannot regret this too much because the money generated by such actions does make the world economy keep moving. There are ways, however, as we have seen, to make mutually beneficial services pay for themselves (see Community Currencies, p. 179).

For centuries the world's religions have warned us of the spiritual dangers of self-indulgence and over-consumption. Quite apart from the physical damage – depleting the finite resources of Earth or causing hardship to the have-nots in the world – voracious consumers who devour more than they need, glutting their taste as well as their appetites, are committing spiritual mayhem. The still small voices of the religious still vouch for small. Doing without is good for your soul, for your fellow humans, and for the planet. Simple living is the best defense.

19

Simpler than Thou

More than for one's time of need,
one needs a God for giving thanks.
— Elias Canetti

Like people who quit smoking, those who have known one way of life and given it up for another are most rabid in their recommendations: "Learn the error of your ways! Do what I have done. Give up your foolish behavior and join me in my happy, free, healthy mode of living!" In my case, simple living. Not that it's all that simple. Nice, though.

My rural retreat is pine-scented, rock-strewn and water-blessed. Myriad lakes, large and small, inhabited and un-, formed by the passing of that mighty glacier, sparkle now in the late summer sun as I write. Thousands of people rush to them in the holiday season. I live on one of them full time. I have already described my paring down process. In spite of my ducks, a warning to those who think that delousing is permanent, I am lighter than I used to be, freed from the weight of things and their accompanying responsibility. (I always hated polishing silver.) City folk who once questioned my sanity now ask me with some respect (or is it awe?) do I like it, and was it a big adjustment? Yes, thank you, and yes, a number of adjustments.

For one thing I had to get used to beauty every day. That was hard, to learn not to stagger under the waves of pleasure that wash over me whenever I look out of my windows. We have been told that the Inuit have 20 to 30 different words for snow, and Newfoundlanders for fog/mist. You'd think Canadians with all their lakes would have at least as many words to describe water. I know an Italian phrase used to describe sunlight dancing on water reflected on a ceiling (it could only have originated in Venice), but how do you describe a similar refraction on a glass-topped table? I'll have to get into fiber optics.

As if shimmering water were not enough to bear, ice shatters me. No one ever told me about winter, when a full moon transforms the ice below into a silver pathway for the stars. And oh, the silence! Early in the morning and late at night, when the motors subside, the loudest noises I hear are the soft swish of my ballpoint on paper, and the click of my thoughts as they come unstuck from the roof of my mind. In his book *Walden*, Thoreau describes a July evening: "A slight sound at evening lifts me up by the ears, and makes life seem inexpressibly serene and grand." Yes, indeed – serene and grand. How blessed I am, lifted up by the ears.

I don't always stay home. The machinery of life requires my forays into town for groceries and stamps. A friend once commented to me that New York is a 12-to-20-block city and Toronto a three-to-five. My little town is a cross-the-street place, and you don't drop $20 in parking fees when you go to do your errands, a practical pleasure. I read a definition of a small town, that it's where you don't have to signal a turn because everyone knows where you're going anyway. Yes, except summer weekends, when I let the city folk know what I'm doing as their numbers force me to turn into the (free) parking lot behind the bank.

I like the simplicity of the lone local grocery store and the classic Aristotelian rules it imposes on my shopping habits. If I want English muffins I must buy them on Thursday because that's when they come in; I go early on spring weekends for fresh asparagus before it's snapped up. I have learned to beat the fall hunters to the soup bones, and the crosscountry skiers to the dried beans. I do stop occasionally for exotic food items at a

Toronto superstore on my way home, but it takes too long. I can pick up a pound of butter at my store and be done with it. At the superstore butter comes in sticks or blocks, salted or un-, lightly churned, whipped, or mixed half and half with margarine. Never mind if the cows are contented, you have to choose their nationality: Danish, British, Canadian. I can't stand the decisions. Butter is just one example. As I become increasingly simple-minded, I find shopping plazas and superstores to be blatant temples of consumerism.

Used to be I was occasionally caught at the checkout counter with no wallet or check book. Without comment, I was handed a counter-check from my bank (the only one in town), no I.D. necessary, or, more commonly (though it doesn't happen often), just told to pay next time. This doesn't happen anymore, as Interac makes trustworthy citizens of us all. The local post office gives me the best service and loving care I have ever had in my life. The mail bag closes at 4:30 p.m. If I'm working down to the wire of a deadline I can call Pamela at 4:15 p.m. and say, "Don't shut the bag, I'm coming in with a Priority Post," secure in the knowledge that my manuscript will be on time. On the other hand, the couriers know the way to my place and usually have a question about what I'm writing now.

Before I moved, someone asked me, "Are you going to buy a gun?"

Shocked, I looked at my American friend, believing that only someone from another country would make that the first question upon being informed that I intended to live year round on a small lake in the Muskokas. Never!

Since I moved in my most powerful weapon has been a broom. I stamp my feet and say "Shoo" to the marauding raccoons who wake me at 3 a.m. step-dancing on my deck. I had a young (two-year-old) bear on the deck last spring going after the birds' suet, and I must admit that got my adrenaline going, but you can't shoot bears here. I called Ben Roberts and he told me to bang pot lids till he got there. He helped me encourage the bear to go down the way he'd come instead of taking a shortcut through my house and he shot a rifle into the air to warn the creature not to come back – once he'd reached the ground safely and scampered away. I had to scrub my windows (with vinegar and newspaper) after it had left to clean off the messy paw prints.

I must admit to more serious acts of violence: I kill mice. In a trap. But it's them or me – my cashmere sweaters, my silk undershirts and me. Mice don't like polyester and I can't say that I blame them. Anyway, I can't afford to replace my warm clothes so I have to make the mice leave the hard way. Now squirrels are getting into the new add-under which is unfinished and very accessible. I stuff mothballs into the insulation to discourage them but they go bowling with them.

Since I seem to be on the subject of wildlife, take ants – and you can, as far as you like. I never knew that ants are among the first harbingers of spring. There must have been an anthill under the cottage. As soon as the weather starts to change, ants appear, ambling across my computer, scurrying across my printer, cluttering up the bathroom. (My bathroom is very small.) It didn't take long to develop a cool head, a clear eye, and a hair-trigger reaction. We all know that one is changed by one's environment. I knew that intellectually; I had to learn it emotionally by living in a small cottage by a lake.

By the end of my first summer, I awed my grandchildren (and my sons-in-law) with my skill at casually squishing an ant with my bare thumb and forefinger and with the kind of nonchalant courage I could have developed only in the wilds of Ontario. (Inwardly I apologized to Albert Schweitzer every time I did this.) I have found that honey works better than poison to get rid of ants, and you don't have to worry about your (grand)children. An open jar of honey attracts all the ants in the neighborhood and you can evict them altogether without resorting to murder. Pioneer's tip.

I also impressed my children with my improved wind and stamina. It's 53 steps down to the lake from the cottage. Coming back up, that's about your average climb to the street from the subway. Every summer I go into training and I get so I can do it carrying life jackets or oars, food or a grandchild (I stopped after they reached age three) and never stop talking. In the winter I get my exercise shoveling snow (just the walks and steps, not the driveway) and carrying wood for my fireplace.

Walking on the water (frozen water, on crosscountry skis) or on deep snow (on snowshoes) are excellent activities. Some people are addicted to snowmobiles but they are noisy and expensive and not much exercise. (Did you know it's possible to take a snowmobile on trails from the Muskokas to Ottawa?) My son John likes to ice-climb and seeks out nice sheer rock-faces covered with sheet ice to add to the hazard. I stopped wanting to know what this boy was doing out of my sight when he was seven. He named a nearby ice cliff after me: Mother's Cliff, and the adjacent climb is called Jocasta. They're both in the Alpine Club Guide Book for Ontario. The trails, by the way, well kept by the snowmobile association and marked with blazes, are wonderful for winter hiking. Given a rotten sense of direction like mine, you wouldn't attempt these without an unerring companion. Forget the blazes: if it's possible for me to go awry, I will. It isn't easy, it's a skill honed by years of trial and error, mostly error.

One of the major skills a writer must have, in addition to a certain facility with words and a polite but strict acquaintance with grammar, is the ability to sit still for hours on end. I think this talent must be genetic; my mother had it, perhaps even to a greater extent than I. (She used to say it made her tired to watch me work.) Anyway, I bless her for this legacy. It's a necessary skill to develop if you plan to live more simply.

I offer you all these details further to prepare you for the simple life. Winter is not quite as simple as summer, at least not in a northern climate. I adore blizzards, when I'm not out in them. Ice storms are bliss, if I'm not driving. I do love being snowed in. What bad weather does best is keep me chained to my chair.

"Oh, goody!" I say. "A storm. What a lovely day to stay in and write!"

Warm weather and summer sunshine are not as good, really, because they make me feel guilty and lure me outside when I might be working. However, I have learned to put up with them. All year round, the silence and solitude are gifts by which a spirit may grow, simply.

I know that I'm probably safer here than in a high-rise in the heart of the city. Although there are only about nine other households resident year-round on my lake, my neighbors across the bay from me can see my lights across the water and know when I'm working late. My nearest neighbor used to be an electrician who made house calls, but he moved. So sometimes I have to call Ben Roberts, at the end of the lake, to find out whether the power failure is something I've done or area-wide. I like power failures, up to a point. I am told that the year before I moved up, there was a power failure on Christmas Day – for nine hours. Cold turkey.

More and more people are coming up to their cottages for Thanksgiving and sometimes Christmas, more often New Year's Eve, and they can tell you exactly how many hours it takes to warm a mattress with an electric blanket. But more and more people are also getting the idea of year-round living, thinking they will simplify their lives by moving out of the city. They're adding on (or under) and insulating and installing all the civilized comforts. There are times I fear that I'll find myself living in an exurban retirement village.

But maybe not. I met someone from a nearby lake who said she and her husband were making tentative retirement plans for their summer place. "What do you do in the winter?" she asked. That's like pricing yachts: if you have to ask, don't.

Remember we're aiming for the simple life, not merely frugal or healthful, but simple, also spiritually enriching. I think the trend toward simple living has become another upper middle-class fad, the in-thing to do, having less to do with things of the spirit than with money-saving tricks and smart investments to keep you off the treadmill. Someone who is intent on saving money can be just as materialistic as someone who is lavishly spending it. To many of these people thrift is a game. They crow about a bargain they picked up at a flea market and use their money-saving coupons as religiously as communion cards, but then they go and buy a $5,000 digital sound system, which makes me wonder how much they've changed. If they try to maintain their former lifestyle and add a rustic cabin to their possessions, they only increase the pressure on themselves and their families. I've seen duplex notepads for people like this, one column headed City, the other headed Country. L.L. Bean Bags were made for them, and very large laundry baskets.

Then there are the one-step-at-a-time people, careful, not too keen on change but willing to make a few concessions because really, things are getting a bit hectic and the money, well, yes, the money is a problem, and it would be nice to slow down, so maybe it might be worth it to cut back a bit, take a deep breath, make a small change, just one, just for fun, see what happens.

A light-hearted but sincere intention to make minor adjustments to daily routines can become heavy with significance. You begin with small offerings and easy deprivations and discover that persistence leads to steadfastness; scarcity carries one through self-denial to selflessness; conscious sacrifices breed grace. You think you're simply down-sizing a little; you find yourself up-shifting a lot. Suddenly you find yourself on a spiritual journey, and it feels good. What they don't tell you in the marketplace, the hucksters and the planners who are trying to force you onward and upward to a brave new world, is that this kind of spiritual striving actually reduces stress.

Want another list to get you started?

- Keep a journal. My favorite recommendation.
- Give something away today.
- Don't buy something today.
- Reach out and help someone. Today.
- Ask someone for help.
- Go for a walk.
- Find a nice place, a hill or a room with a view. Enjoy.
- Is this a good time and place to meditate? So meditate.
- Get organized. Start with a list.
- Throw the list away and start another one.
- Choose one thing on your list and do it, or start doing it.
- Forgive someone today. (Guaranteed to relieve tension.)
- Listen to someone today – your mate? your child/children? your mother? (Yes!)
- Do something today you've never done before. This could be as simple as walking down a street you've never walked before or as complicated as starting a new religion. Either way, you'll change your perspective.
- Let go. And there's a corollary to this sentence for those who are comfortable with it –
- Let God.

20

Enough Already!

There must be more to life than having everything.
– Maurice Sendak

We know all the fables and parables told to us over the centuries, their point perfectly clear. King Midas discovered that a genuine tear on his daughter's cheek was worth more than all his gold. We know that. Why is it that every generation has to reinvent the merry-go-round and waste time trying to discover how to get off? How is it we never learn the neverending lesson that soulless accumulation teaches? This time round we make jokes about it. Cynics have taken over the bromides of the ages and changed the lines, made puns of them all, and not only the punch lines suffer. We have become cliché-phobic. If Aesop were alive today, even he would have trouble finding a moral. We've heard all the wise aphorisms, though we seem unable to learn them – learn them well enough to live by them, that is.

Before we can change our behavior we have to change our attitudes; before we can change our attitudes we have to change our psyches, before we can change our psyches, we have to understand them – ourselves.

Consider the psychology of money. Some folks can't ever get enough. I used to think this was an attitude left over from the Depression because I first observed it in my parents' generation. Later I saw it in the Boomers, the kids

– adults now – whom I helped bring into the world and who married mine, the ones who love new, expensive, technological toys, who made Bill Gates what he is today and who think the solution to almost any problem can be bought. But now I see the attitude persisting even through the X Generation unto the youngsters. Some people are born empty, that's all there is to it.

No matter how much money or security they have, they'll go on feeling that way – empty. These are the ones who load their freezers and cupboards with food, their closets with clothes, their houses with goods and stuff. These are the ones for whom shopping malls were created, whose idea of entertainment, culture, or travel is bringing home the *tchotchkes*. This is still the most prevalent North American attitude to money today, I think, encouraged by Madison Avenue and most governments, though it's getting harder and harder to sustain.

The problem is that everything costs more now so they're scrambling to keep body and soul, as well as the home, together. Surveys have indicated that if every woman working outside the home quit tomorrow, the number of families living below the poverty line would double. Define poverty line. That's one of the tasks facing us: figuring out what poverty is. Which way and how far is down? Where, exactly, is the bottom line? We must not forget that bottom lines are set higher than they used to be, except in Third World countries. Take a quick look at your own spending habits and those of your parents. Compare what you think is necessity and what an earlier generation thought of as luxury.

Then there is the growing threat of psychological poverty. Some people never get enough stuff while others can never squirrel away enough money. They feel poorest when they're spending it. This, I used to think, was a real depression-fostered attitude, the compulsion to pinch pennies and scrounge and scavenge and let others pick up the tab and never give an inch (Brother, can you paradigm?), but then I realized that you'll always see people who hold back – money or themselves – fearing that they're going to be short-changed, cut out, left high and dry, and of course they are, how could they not be? Fear of poverty is almost worse than poverty because nothing can assuage it. You know you're poor if you have nothing to give others.

Children who are fed a little and clothed somewhat, but inadequately compared to their peers, suffer from this. So do Third World people with access to a television set. The disparity between what they see and what they haven't got is too vast. Kids don't press their noses against the glass of the candy store window anymore; they press it against the television screen. People don't salivate for a stick of candy; they slaver for a slice of the world's pie. Everyone who decides to down (or up) shift has to be uncomfortably aware of the huge gaps in lifestyles. If we believe, as most of the world's religions hold, that we are in some way our siblings' keepers, then we must all take very seriously our responsibility for our human family members, and that includes seeing to a more equitable dispersal and use of money.

We count our precious, hard-earned dollars, be they metal or paper currency, and the statement is clear on them that they are legal tender, indicating the responsibility of our country's government for their and our value. We reveal with our use of money how we feel not only about our country but about ourselves and our fellow humans. Faith, hope and charity, these three, but the greatest of all is money, the possession of which makes possible all other goods and services. If money did not exist, someone would have to have invented it and of course, someone did, and has, several times. Community currencies (see p. 179) are simply a new expression of an old need: solvency, or is it survival?

Aside from generic attitudes to money, there are also gender attitudes to take into account. I have written in another book of the difference in money attitudes between males and females. Most men consider money to be a power tool, a practical means to a larger goal, that of making more money. The ones with the most expensive toys win. Most women see money as a security blanket. They use money for immediate ends: to feed their families and to educate their children. The buck doesn't stop with them long enough to get warm. Gradually now, women are beginning to learn men's lesson: that money can be employed to generate more money, thus assuring not only present comfort but future security. The United Nations Fourth World Conference on Women held in Beijing in 1995 suggested that if the women of the world were given credit for their contribution to the GDP of their countries, granted the opportunity to be educated, and ceded access to enough means or land to enable them to feed their families – what? The world would be a better place? It almost goes without saying except that there was another world survey, the World Population Council, also in 1995, which was trying to discover, among other things, whether women are going to become more like men and abandon their commitment to their children.

Being happy is analogous to that old line about being rich. If you have to ask how much something costs, you can't afford it. So, if you have to ask whether you're happy, don't ask. Happiness can't be summoned or legislated; it sneaks up on you. It's a by-product, springing from your hands, or head or heart or eyes, whatever you happen to be doing. An ephemeral epiphany (I like that). The columnist Russell Baker once said that there's more happiness in a bottle of good wine than anyone can bear, or deserves, or needs – something like that. Maybe I said it. We all say much the same thing, once we're on track. We recommend compassion, tolerance, justice, integrity, simplicity, not because we're nerds or nuts or bores but because these are the ways to peace, inner and outer, and simplicity. How we long to go through the eye of the needle and not be dragging our threads behind us.

These are some of the attitudes and facts that I have considered as I tried to figure out how much we can afford to change (how can we afford not to?), to simplify our lifestyles and bring them more into alignment with a world standard of living. The old chicken-in-every-pot idea (the New Deal campaign slogan that put FDR in the White House during the Depression) has been enlarged to the idealistic belief that no one should have two homes until everyone has one. I say idealistic because it's such a long way from reality today.[1] Add to an increasingly uncomfortable conscience a nagging worry about the health of the planet (greenhouse effect, thinning of the ozone layer, air pollution, dwindling of fossil fuels and other nonrenewable resources, depletion of fish stocks, and so on) and you begin to understand why people are beginning to shift - uneasily.

Even with controlled media stories that don't tell us everything, we cannot but notice the hideous discrepancy between the haves and have-nots of this century. According to the United Nations' Human Development Report 1996, the combined wealth of the world's 358 billionaires equals the total income of the poorest 45 percent of the world's population, some 2.3 billion people.[2] Surely it is not too much to say that this is inequitable. Only gullible governments who listen to the corporate myth-makers buy the story that unmitigated, uncontrolled economic growth is good for everyone. There's a credibility gap that's hard to close when we see so patently that it's bad for the planet and for the people in Third World countries trying to cope with the hideous aftermath of industrial "improvements." Feeling hopeless and helpless, even as the previously affluent North American middle class is dwindling, we cling to the Zen belief in the power of a butterfly's wing.

Oh, that butterfly! The lovely creature with the powerful wing is supposed to cause with one sweep a tidal wave on the other side of the planet. Is it possible? Do we dare to believe it?

Believe it. Don't try to tear the wing off to analyze it. Believing that our individual actions do and can make a difference, we begin to restructure our lives and lifestyles, hoping to save ourselves as well as the planet. How do we begin? Quietly, voluntarily, simply.

Appendix 1

Some Interesting Organizations and Addresses

Alternatives for Simple Living
A nonprofit organization whose mission is to "equip people of faith to challenge consumerism, live justly, and celebrate responsibly." They have developed a variety of resources and publish a catalogue.
3617 Old Lakeport Rd., P.O. Box 2857, Sioux City, IA 51106
1–800–821–6153.

Canadian Association for Media Education British Columbia (CAME)
Co-ordinator Mary Ungerleider
1363 Fountain Way, Vancouver, BC V6H 3T2, E-mail: *maryu@wimsey.com*

Context Institute
Since 1979, CI, a nonprofit research organization, has been exploring and clarifying what is involved in a human sustainable culture, and how to get it.
http://context.org/
They also publish *In Context: A Quarterly of Humane Sustainable Culture*, a journal of hope, sustainability and change.
E-mail: *ci@context.org*

The Cultural Environment Movement (CEM)
P.O. Box 3187, Philadelphia, PA 19104

Friends of the Earth
The largest international network of environmental groups in the world (in 52 countries)
E-mail: *webmaster@foe.co.uk*

The Greater Vancouver Regional District
4330 Kingsway, Burnaby, BC V5H 4G8
http://www.gvrd.bc.ca/shoes/publ-info.html

Green-Net, Association for Progressive Communications
APC is a global computer network for change, dedicated to serving non-governmental organizations and citizen activists working for social change. In Canada it's known as the Canadian Co-operative Association (CCA). The addresses are
The Association for Progressive Communications,
Presidio Bldg. 1012, First Floor, Torney Ave., P.O. Box 29904-0904, San Francisco, CA 94129-0904, E-mail: *apcadmin@apc.org*
AND
Canadian Co-operative Association
275 Bank St., Suite 400, Ottawa, ON K2P 2L6, phone: 613–238–6711
http://www.energ.polimi.it/development/ORG/di144.htm

Ithaca Hours
Home Money Starter Kit $25 (US). "Hour Town," 20-minute video, $15 (US).
Paul Glover, Box 6578, Ithaca, NY 14851
E-mail: *hours@lightlink.com,*
http://www.publiccom.com/web/ithacahour/

The Lead Pencil Club
P.O. Box 380, Wainscott, NY 11975

The Media Foundation (TMF)
see *Adbusters,* below

New Luddites:
Challenging the legitimacy of science and technology (1796–1998)
"The New Luddites are a dis-organization. That means no distant leadership, no formal membership, no AGMs and no subs. If you agree with our aims, you are welcome."
E-mail: *socs203@york.ac.uk*

The New Road Map Foundation
P.O. Box 15981, Seattle, WA 98115
http://www.scn.org/earth/lightly/vsnuroad.htm

The Nuclear Age Peace Foundation
An International Education and Advocacy Group on Issues of International Peace and Security, a global network comprised of more than 850 citizen action groups.
http://www.wagingpeace.org/index.html

Phinney Neighborhood Association
6532 Phinney Ave. N., Seattle, WA 98102, E-mail: *PNACenter@aol.com*

The Pierce Simplicity Study
http://www.mbay.net/~pierce/

E. F. Schumacher Society
140 Jug End Road, Great Barrington, MA 01230
http://members.aol.com/efssociety

Simple Living Network
Support Groups and Study Circles, *http://www.slnet.com/*

Social Investment Organization (SIO)
366 Adelaide St. E., Suite 443, Toronto, ON M5A 3X9
E-mail: *sio@web.net*

Sustainable Seattle
Metrocenter YMCA — 909 4th Ave., Seattle, WA 98104
E-mail: *sustea@halcyon.com*

WICEN
Women in Co-operatives Electronic Network is an electronic discussion group open to women and men who share an interest in issues involving women in co-operatives, and credit.
http://www.wisc.edu/uwcc/info/wicen.html

World Stewardship Institute
409 Mendocino Ave., Suite A, Santa Rosa, CA 95401-8513

Worldwatch Institute,
1776 Massachusetts Ave., N.W., Washington, DC 20036
E-mail: *wwpub@worldwatch.org*

Publications, Journals and Zines

Adbusters
"Dedicated to reinventing the outdated paradigms of our consumer culture and building a brave new understanding of living," and published by The Media Foundation. *http://www.adbusters.org/info/Foundation.html*
To subscribe to *Adbusters* (1 year/4 issues – $20),
call toll-free 1–800–663–1243, or fax 604–737–6021,
or visit *http://www.adbusters.org/Subs/subscription/html*
Price is in Canadian dollars; add 7% GST to Canadian orders.

Alternatives
An independent Canadian environmental quarterly journal now in its 26th year. Faculty of Environmental Studies, University of Waterloo, Waterloo, ON N2L 3G1, *http://www.fes.uwaterloo.ca/Research/Alternatives/*
E-mail: *alternat@fes.uwaterloo.ca*

Balancing Act
$12/yr. (12 issues), 84 Tarbox Street, Dedham, MA 02026

Beer Frame
The key to this one is in the subtitle: *Journal of Inconspicuous Consumption.*
It is described as "a field guide to deriving maximum pleasure from a
minimum of resources," one of the most popular zines around. To order a
copy, write Paul Lukas at *consumer@interport.net* or
160 St. John's Place, Brooklyn, NY 11217

BWZine
The online better world magazine.
http://www.betterworld.com/BWZ/9606/index.htm

The Cheapskate Monthly
$18/yr. (12 issues), P.O. Box 2135, Paramount, CA 90723-8135
http://www.cheapsk8.com/cmbooks.html

Community Economics
Ontario's only newsletter on community economic development: 134
Spadina Ave., Ste. 402, Toronto, ON fax. 416-703-0552. An individual
subscription is $16.05/yr. (GST included). Previous copies $2.14 each. But
here's a neat thing: "Green Dollars through the Toronto LETSystem are
accepted for 50% of the cost. Account 3579."
http://www.web.net/~osdcoff/comecon/issuesl.htm

Country Connections magazine
"Plus 2 extra-page bonus issues on special topics," $22/yr. (6 issues)
Dept. WW, 14431 Ventura Bl, #407, Sherman Oaks, CA 91423
It also publishes a pamphlet: *A Guide to Getting Out and Getting a Decent
Life: Practical advice and helpful resources toward personal change.*
http//www.igc.apc.org/cocomag

Discounts Newsletter
HOT LINKS: over 300 links to moneysaving sites.
http://www.clis.com/savvynews/ldefault.htm

The Dollar Stretcher
A free weekly newsletter. To subscribe send E-mail to *gary@stretcher.com* with "subscribe" in the subject and your E-mail address in the body of the letter.

Ecolution
(Conscious Consumer Guide), P.O. Box 2279, Merrifield, VA 22116
http://ecolution.com/conscious.html

EcoNews
"On Wealth, Waste and What We Really Want," published every month as a service to the Vancouver Island community, funded by readers' donations. Send check to EcoNews, 2069 Kings Rd., Victoria, BC V8R 2P6

The Frugal Gazette
P.O. Box 3395, Newtown, CT 06470-3395
http://www.frugalgazette.com/email.htm

The GreenMoney Journal
$35/yr., *http://www.greenmoney.com/index.html*
– or use a credit card through the *Simple Living Network* at 1-800-318-5725.

Home Equity Conversion:
The Study of Reverse Mortgages as a Housing and Planning Option
Cost $8. The booklet describes reverse mortgages and compares different plans. It lists details of various products available in Canada and provides a checklist of questions consumers should ask when purchasing a reverse mortgage, focusing on the costs involved. For a copy contact
The Public Interest Advocacy Center, 1 Nicholas St., Suite 410, Ottawa, ON K1N 7B7

International Journal of Community Currency Research
Volume 1, 1997, *http://www.lmu.ac.uk/dbe/cudem/ijccr/ltoc.htm*

Journal of Voluntary Simplicity
Published quarterly by Simple Living Press; subscriptions in the US are $16; in Canada $21 (US); all other countries $24(US). Order a sample for $5 or subscription by placing an order on-line: *http://simpleliving.com/subscrib.htm* or call toll-free: 1–800–318–5725. Back issues (if not out of print) are available by sending check or money order to: Simple Living, 2319 N. 45th St., Box 149, Seattle, WA 98103

Living Gently Quarterly
$20/yr. (4 issues), P.O. Box 8302, Victoria, BC V8W 3R9
E-mail: *see@islandnet.com*

The Miser's Gazette
A Home Page from Ian Nicholson, Canada's #1 Miser,
http://www.ctsnet.com/miser/

New Horizons Journal
"The way we work subscriptions is this: We add your E-mail address to a notification list. When a new issue is posted on the Web we notify you by E-mail. We can send copies of back issues free if sent over the Internet by E-mail. You will need a Web Browser to read the contents."
E-mail to: *nhorizons@aol.com*
http://users.aol.com/nhorizons/journal.htm

101 Ways to Reuse your Old Shoes 'N Other Stuff: A Money-Saving Guide to Reusing, Repairing, and Renting Goods in the Lower Mainland.
Available from the Greater Vancouver Regional District
http://www.grvd.bc.ca E-mail: *webmaster@grvd.bc.ca*

Plain
Described by Bill Henderson as "a low-tech magazine that will soothe your electronically jangled soul."
The Center for Plain Living, P.O. Box 100, Chesterhill, OH 43728

Savvy Discounts Newsletter
Free sample issue of newsletter (US orders only; only persons 18 years or older), *http://www.clis.com/savvynews/ldefault.htm*
E-mail: *savvynews@bmd.cllis.com*

Simple Living News
$20/yr. (10 issues), Box 1884, Jonesboro, GA 30337-1884
E-mail: *kilgo@mindspring.com*

Simple Living Quarterly
$14/yr. (4 issues), 2319 N. 45th Street, Box 149, Seattle, WA 98013
http://simpleliving.com/subscrib.htm

Skinflint News
$12/yr. (12 issues), Box 818, Palm Harbor, FL 34683-5639

Thrift SCORE
$5/5 issues (cask or check payable to Al Hoff), Box 90282, Pittsburgh, PA 15224, E-mail: *hoffo@drycas.club.cc.cmu.edu*

Traders & Recyclers Directory
ReUse Market, 43 Speedvale Ave. W., Guelph, ON N1H 1J5

Other Useful Information, with URLs and/or E-mail Addresses

Back to Walden Pond
The Henry David Thoreau Campfire Chat
http://www.kildevilhill.com/waldenpondchat/wwwboard.html

Co-operative Car Network – Vancouver
A not-for-profit co-operative incorporated to promote car sharing as an economically beneficial and environmentally responsible transportation option to private car ownership.
http://www.eagletree.com/think/bettertransport.html

The Socially Responsible (SRB) Discussion Group
To subscribe, send an E-mail to the SRB List with nothing except the words: "subscribe srb your name (e.g. "subscribe srb BJ Wylie")
E-mail: *sio@web.apc.org*

For a list of Memorial Societies in Canada
http://vbiweb.champlain.edu/famsa/drectryc.htm

Appendix 2

If the World Were a Village
– by Donella H. Meadows

Value Earth Poster
available for $7 (US) postpaid from Value Earth, c/o David Copeland, 707 White Horse Pike, C-2, Absecon, NJ 08201 fx. 609-272-1571

If the world were a village of 1,000 people, it would include
584 Asians
124 Africans
95 East and West Europeans
84 Latin Americans
55 Russians (including for the moment Lithuanians, Latvians, Estonians, and other national groups)
52 North Americans
6 Australians and New Zealanders.

The people of the village have considerable difficulty in communicating:
165 people speak Mandarin
86 English
83 Hindu/Urdu
64 Spanish
58 Russian
37 Arabic.
That list accounts for the mother tongues of only half the villagers. The other half speak (in descending order of frequency) Bengali, Portuguese, Indonesian, Japanese, German, French, and 200 other languages.

In the village of 1,000 there are
329 Christians (Among them 187 Catholics, 84 Protestants, 31 Orthodox)
178 Moslems
167 "non-religious"
132 Hindus
60 Buddhists
45 atheists
3 Jews
86 all other religions.

One-third (330) of the 1,000 people in the world village are children and only 60 are over the age of 65. Half the children are immunized against preventable infectious diseases such as measles and polio.

Just under half the married women in the village have access to and use modern contraceptives.

The first year 28 babies are born. That year 10 people die, 3 of them for lack of food, 1 from cancer; 2 of the deaths are of babies born within the year. One person of the 1,000 is infected with the HIV virus; that person most likely has not yet developed a full-blown case of AIDS.

With the 28 births and 10 deaths, the population of the village in the second year is 1,018.

In the 1,000-person community, 200 people receive 75 percent of the income; another 200 receive only 2 percent of the income.

Only 70 people of the 1,000 own an automobile (though some of the 70 own more than one automobile).

About one-third have access to clean, safe drinking water.

Of the 670 adults in the village, half are illiterate. [of the illiterate, 86 percent are women. BJW]

The village has six acres of land per person, 6,000 acres in all, of which
700 acres are cropland
1,400 acres are pasture
1,900 acres are woodland
2,000 acres desert, tundra, pavement and other wasteland.

The woodland is declining rapidly; the wasteland is increasing. The other land categories are roughly stable.

The village allocates 83 percent of its fertilizer to 40 percent of its cropland – that owned by the richest and best-fed 270 people. Excess fertilizer running off this land causes pollution in lakes and wells. The remaining 60 percent of the land, with its 17 percent of the fertilizer, produces 28 percent of the food grains and feeds for 73 percent of the people. The average grain yield on that land is one-third the harvest achieved by the richer villagers.

In the village of 1,000 people there are
5 soldiers
7 teachers
1 doctor
3 refugees driven from home by war or drought.

The village has a total budget each year, public and private, of over $3 million – $3,000 per person if it is distributed evenly (which, we have already seen, it isn't).

Of the total $3 million
$181,000 goes to weapons and warfare
$159,000 for education
$132,000 for health care.

The village has buried beneath it enough explosive power in nuclear weapons to blow itself to smithereens many times over. These weapons are under the control of just 100 of the people. The other 900 people are watching them with deep anxiety, wondering whether they can learn to get along together; and if they do, whether they might set off the weapons anyway through inattention or technical bungling; and, if they ever decide to dismantle the weapons, where in the world village they would dispose of the radioactive materials of which the weapons are made.

– quoted from *The Millennium Whole Earth Catalog* (HarperSanFrancisco, 1994)

Shakertown Pledge[2]

Recognizing that Earth and the fullness thereof is a gift from our gracious God, and that we are called to cherish, nurture, and provide loving stewardship for Earth's resources, and recognizing that life itself is a gift, and a call to responsibility, joy, and celebration, I make the following declarations:

1. I declare myself to be a world citizen.
2. I commit myself to lead a life of creative simplicity and to share my personal wealth with the world's poor.
3. I commit myself to join with others in the reshaping of institutions in order to bring about a more just global society in which all people have full access to the needed resources for their physical, emotional, intellectual, and spiritual growth.
4. I commit myself to occupational accountability, and so doing I will seek to avoid the creation of products which cause harm to others.
5. I affirm the gift of my body and commit myself to its proper nourishment and physical well-being.
6. I commit myself to examine continually my relations with others, and to attempt to relate honestly, morally, and lovingly to those around me.

7. I commit myself to personal renewal through prayer, meditation, and study.

8. I commit myself to responsible participation in a community of faith.

Endnotes

Chapter 1

[1] Quoted from the Indian journal *Visva-Bharati Quarterly*, August 1936.

Chapter 2

[1] from "The Death of the Middle Class," by Daphne Bramhan and Gordon Hamilton, in *Transition*, March 1993.

[2] Matthew 19:16–24; Matthew 6:25–30.

[3] Another guru who has Web sites devoted to him. The author of the 1973 book *Small Is Beautiful: Economics as if People Mattered* is the inspiration behind the current E. F. Schumacher Society, and the second annual Decentralist Conference which took place in June, 1997.

[4] A meme is a unit of cultural meaning, most commonly picked up from too much television. Oxford zoologist Richard Dawkins, also responsible for the idea of the "selfish gene," theorizes that trivia and pop culture can be compared to viruses in their rapid replication. cf. Douglas Rushkoff's *Media Virus!* which presents the idea that today's media are hosts carrying new memes. You can see how important it is to resist if you are going to be yourself.

Chapter 3

[1] *Gage Canadian Dictionary*, Copyright 1983 by Gage Educational Publishing Company.

[2] taken from Paul Dickson's, *The Official Rules* (New York: Delacorte Press, 1978).

[3] "You might say Dr. Richard Buggeln is an alchemist: he is helping Tennesseans turn straw into gold." Mike Bradley in *Tennessee Alumnus*, Winter 1996.

[4] Quoted from a Fact Sheet distributed on the Internet, an article entitled "Living in a Material World," by Laura McCarty, June 1994.

[5] *Simplify Your Life* (New York: Hyperion, 1994); *Inner Simplicity* (New York: Hyperion, 1995); *Living the Simple Life* (New York: Hyperion, 1996).

Chapter 4

[1] op. cit.

Chapter 5

[1] Dr. George Gerbner, from the 15-year survey of television that he conducted.
[2] Taken from a piece about media literacy.
    http://www.igc.apc.org/mef/about.html
[3] Source: *National Coalition on Television Violence*.
[4] This figure varies according to which survey or expert you read. The American Psychological Association estimates that the average American child or teenager views 10,000 acts of violence *per year* on television.
[5] From a lecture by Dr. George Gerbner to Science for Peace, Toronto, July 14, 1995, sponsored by Science for Peace and C-CAVE (Canadians - Concern about Violence in Entertainment), and reprinted on Web site http://www.web.apc.org/~pgs/pages/gerb714.html

Chapter 6

[1] Published in New Zealand as *Counting for Nothing: What Men Value and What Women Are Worth*. See bibliography for information on the American edition.

Chapter 7

[1] Did you know that in the last century, when the pioneer women were writing their diaries or letters home, they would write down the page, give it a quarter turn and write across what they had written, and if they had more to say, give it another quarter turn and write some more? Very hard on the eyes.

Chapter 8

[1] *Gage Canadian Dictionary*, Copyright 1983 by Gage Educational Publishing Company.
[2] See Christmas Gift Vouchers, p. 172
[3] *Minutes of the Lead Pencil Club* (Wainscott, NY: Pushcart Press, 1996).
[4] A Christmas Gift Exemption Voucher is a coupon you hand out to your friends and family which exempts them from spending money *on* you, conditional on their spending time *with* you.
[5] Quoted in *The Millennium Whole Earth Catalog: Access to Tools & Ideas for the Twenty-First Century*, edited by Howard Rheingold, (New York: HarperSanFrancisco, Copyright 1994 by Point Foundation).

Chapter 9

[1] From a February 5, 1997, speech given by Ted Turner in New York City, at a lunch sponsored by the American Society of Magazine Editors, quoted in *Harper's*, June 1997.

[2] Robert Browning, in "Andrea del Sarto," 1855.

[3] *Lady Windermere's Fan*, 1892.

[4] *Everywoman's Money Book* (Toronto: Key Porter Books, 1995).

[5] My electricity bill goes from a high of $500-plus in the dead of winter to $60-something in the summer. It makes me feel better to figure out the annual amount and divide by 12. Of course, I have to have the money in my account to pay for the January/February chill.

[6] Note that it would be preferable to contribute to your RRSP as well as to your savings, but if you can't do this at first, start with the RRSP.

[7] At the time of writing, the Canadian government allows you a tax credit of 17 percent of your annual charitable donations up to $200, and 29 percent for anything above that. If you figure on an annual expenditure, you'll know better how to apportion your largesse to the ever-mounting piles of pleas that land in your mailbox every day.

[8] If you are self-employed, you can earn a tax credit on that portion of your house that you use for business purposes.

[9] If you are self-employed, you can get a tax credit for a percentage of your driving which is done for business purposes. You must keep mileage records to document this.

[10] See pages 147-150.

[11] If you're self-employed, as I am, part of eating out goes under entertainment (50 percent tax credit); part goes under travel (for business); and part goes to laziness and take-out.

[12] Some of this can be charged to entertainment, if you're self-employed. Some people make their own wine or beer and even drink it. Lo-alc beer is inexpensive, low-calorie, and tastes good with a sandwich.

[13] The best defense is eating well. Take care of yourself. It's called preventive medicine. Then you won't need too many prescriptions. Antibiotics have lost their power due to over-use. Take a look at a few inexpensive home remedies (p.163).

[14] This list is not as facetious as it sounds. A clone is an assistant, doing whatever it is that wives/mothers/husbands/fathers do but need extra hands for. Sometimes it's cleaning, sometimes shopping, doing the books, making a casserole, picking up the kids or the drycleaning, helping to make costumes for the school pageant, planting the impatiens – you know your clone-needs better than I do. They're hard

to find, for love or money. Elves are also worth their weight in gold. Like Ben Roberts, they cost, but some services can't be paid for, like coming to give moral support when driving a bear off one's deck, or thawing a septic or water line on the coldest day in January, or plowing one's driveway far too early in the morning when one has to drive in to Toronto, or getting one out of a snowdrift when one was blinded by a sudden white-out. Be sure to include elves in your budget, no matter how you trim it. Also fairy godmothers (sometimes called mothers-in-law) – helpful kin or friendly neighbors or faithful baby-sitters who sometimes can't be paid with money but can be showered with gratitude, love, homemade soup and jollies. (Jollies are not presents, as such; they are little gifts to "jolly" life along.)

[15] In my business, these all classify as research and earn tax credits.

[16] "Just 12 easy payments," goes the ad, encouraging you to buy the latest electronic gadget with stereotypical attachments.

Chapter 10

[1] Information taken from a Mutual Fund Tutorial, http://www.quote.com/mutual-funds/tutorial/what.html

[2] Information provided by Bob Darling of Investors' Group.

[3] According to Statistics Canada, the average age of retirement for Canadians has dropped from 66 to 62.

[4] For the Canadian Ethical Investment Web site see http://www.web.net/ethmoney/new.htm.

[5] I have arranged for as much of my income as possible to be deposited directly and for many of my bills to be paid by automatic withdrawal (utilities, telephone, township taxes, car lease, and so on) – a footnote to simplify your life. My planetary worry is that my computer chip has dropped poison into Earth's system. Some things are beyond my control.

[6] This is the no-no that has sent Canadian trappers into poverty and starvation. That's not inhumane?

[7] Does anyone remember that recent fire in a sweatshop in Thailand which none of the employees escaped because all the doors were locked?

Chapter 11

[1] Just to complete the roster, my youngest child, Matthew, the brain-damaged one, needed expensive special schooling for two years at the end of his school career, which I paid for. Looking back, I wonder how I did it.

[2] A woman's top salary now equals about 70 percent of a man's, that is, for a full-time job; part-time jobs, more frequently held by women than by men, still pay only about 60-63 percent of a man's wage.

[3] Ideas suggested by Tim Cestnick in a special to the *Globe and Mail*, August 30, 1997. Tim Cestnick is a CA, president of the Waterstreet Group in Toronto, author of *A Declaration of Taxpayer Rights* (Bateman Financial Consultants, Ltd., Burlington, updated annually).

Chapter 12

[1] The coroner's office refuses to keep track. Arbitrary addresses are assigned, such as the hospital where the deceased died, the last known address, or the nearest street address to the spot where the person died.

[2] See http://www.unl.edu/casestudy/456/leslie.htm

[3] The Perth County Conspiracy was such a group, living on a farm outside of Stratford, Ontario, when I was there. I gave them some of my sourdough bread culture. They actually formed a singing ensemble and cut an lp record. One of the songs praised Perth County Green (marijuana).

[4] Faith Popcorn is the bestselling author of *The Popcorn Report* and Chair of BrainReserve [sic] Inc., a marketing consultancy firm she founded in 1974. *Clicking* (New York: HarperBusiness, 1995) was co-authored with Lys Marigold.

[5] I recommend *The Best Is Yet to Come* (Toronto: Key Porter Books, 1996), co-authored by Christopher Cottier and me.

[6] These last two case histories are taken from Doris Janzen Longacre's book *Living More with Less* (Scottsdale, PA: Herald Press, 1980).

Chapter 13

[1] Could you have foreseen this in the mid-1800s when the automobile was invented? Question Number 63 from Gregory Stock's, *The Book of Questions* (New York: Workman Publishing, 1987).

[2] Here's a tightwad tip about car insurance: a five-year-old car may no longer need comprehensive coverage. And you might want to raise your deductible allowance. It's possible you won't care if you add another dent or two.

[3] I am indebted for her generosity in letting me use her budget template.

[4] My editor takes fervent exception to this. He just traded up from a 1985 Nissan Sentra and a 1982 Toyota pickup to one 10-year-old Nissan Maxima (for $6,000). He says it's in mint condition, with fewer than average miles, purchased not from a little old lady but from a recently retired, fairly well-to-do couple who sold it so they could buy a brand new Maxima (for $38,000). All these transactions, both the sale of his own vehicles and the purchase of the "replacement" (hardly new) car, were accomplished through the classified ads. Anyway, you should know that my editor disagrees with Axelsson. If this book goes into a second edition, I'll tell you what happened to his car.

[5] Quoted from *Wisecracks*, the 1992 National Film Board film about women stand-up comics, directed by Gail Singer.

Chapter 14

[1] Most of these notes (interwoven with my own) come from the Web site of the Funeral and Memorial Societies of America (FAMSA), copyright © FAMSA 1996 (http://www.funerals.org/famsa), who generously allow use of their information with due acknowledgment.

[2] Some 25 different parts of a human being's body can be recycled now, including the kidneys, bones and joints, bone marrow, corneas, brains, heart, lungs, liver, intestines (for research), pancreas, temporal bones (in the ear), pituitary glands, and skin.

[3] If you are worried about being kept alive by extreme (expensive) measures, this document requests that you be allowed to die. You can get a software package (PC compatible), *Standard Living Will*, with the document on disk, ready for you to fill in the blanks. From Software Ltd., Richmond Hill, ON, L4B 2B2.

Chapter 15

[1] "A six-year-old pillow can have a tenth of its weight consist of old skin, mold, dust mites, and dust mite dung. Your mattress can easily harbor two million thriving little critters. The dust mite – specifically an allergen in its droppings – is a proven cause of morning headaches, runny nose, itchy skin and puffy eyes among sufferers of asthma, rhinitis, related respiratory problems and eczema." From a magazine ad.

[2] *Solo Chef* (Toronto: Macmillan Canada, 1997).

[3] These last three tips cut down on impulse purchases.

⁴ These and 500 other time- and money-saving tips are available in a copy of Vicki Lansky's *Baking Soda* book, available for $9.95 plus $2 postage and handling, plus 84 cents GST, for a total of $12.79, from The Leader Co., Inc., Publishing Division, Dept. BK903, P.O. Box 6000, Brampton, Ontario L6V 1V0.

⁵ "Tao of the Dumpster – My father's love affair with trash," by Dirk Jamison, was published in the *Utne Reader* for November-December 1996, reprinted from the *L. A. Weekly* for June 14, 1996. Dirk Jamison is coauthor of *Doing Good*, a book about philosophy and religion, published by William Morrow. At the time of writing this article, he was working on a book about his father and had completed a documentary about him.

⁶ *Management in the Home* (New York: Dodd, Mead & Company, 1959).

Chapter 16

¹ *Gage Canadian Dictionary*, Copyright 1983 by Gage Educational Publishing Company.

² Some of this information was taken from *The Canadian Encyclopedia Plus* (Toronto: McClelland & Stewart, 1996), and from an essay on community currencies by Bernard Leitaer.

³ In *Through the Looking Glass*, by Lewis Carroll.

⁴ This story and information thanks to the E. F. Schumacher Society; an article on local currencies by Robert Swann and Susan Witt, written in February 1955.

⁵ You can buy a kit explaining how to start an Ithaca Hours system. See Appendix 1.

⁶ 100 in Australia, 70 in New Zealand, 400 in England, 50 in Ireland, 20 in Scotland, 100 in Germany, 80 in France, plus about a dozen cities in Canada.

⁷ The exception is that if you are paid credits for something you don't work at as a living, this can be "hobby income" and perhaps not taxable. As with anything else, when in doubt, ask. Check with your friendly neighborhood tax man and find out whether you just got reclassified with a new trade. If you did, then keep track of your expenses; you pay tax only on profits.

Chapter 17

[1] Listed in *Beginnings: A Book for Widows* (Toronto: McClelland & Stewart, 1997).

Chapter 20

[1] I'm sure it will cheer everyone to learn that Barbara Streisand recently cut down by selling five of her seven homes.

[2] Reported in *Utne Reader*, November/December 1996.

Appendix 2

[1] "This pledge was written by a group of religious retreat leaders who felt bad about being members of a privileged minority in a nation guilty of overconsumption of the world's resources. They recognized that their own lifestyles were part of the problem. They named their pledge the Shakertown Pledge in honor of their original gathering place and because the Shaker community had believed wholeheartedly in lives of 'creative simplicity'." Excerpted from *Treasury of Celebrations*, edited by Carolyn Pogue (Kelowna, BC: Northstone Publishing, 1996).

Bibliography

Aslett, Don.
    Clutter's Last Stand.
    Cincinnati, OH: Writer's Digest Books, 1984.

The Beardstown Ladies (with Leslie Whitaker).
    The Beardstown Ladies' Common-Sense Investment Guide.
    New York: Hyperion, 1996.

Breathnach, Sarah Ban.
    Simple Abundance: A Daybook of Comfort and Joy.
    New York: Warner Books, 1995.

Canetti, Elias.
    The Secret Heart of the Clock: Notes, Aphorisms, Fragments 1973–1985.
    New York: Farrar Straus Giroux, 1989.

Csikszentmihalyi, Mihaly.
    Flow: The Psychology of Optimal Experience.
    New York: HarperPerennial, 1990.

—. *The Evolving Self: A Psychology for the Third Millennium.*
    New York: HarperCollins, 1993.

Dacyczyn, Amy.
    The Tightwad Gazette II: Promoting Thrift as a Viable Alternative Lifestyle.
    New York: Villard Books, 1995.

Daly, Steven and Nathaniel Wice.
    alt.culture: and a-to-z guide to the '90s – underground, online, and over-the-counter.
    New York: HarperPerennial, 1995.

Dappen, Andy.
    Cheap Tricks (100s of Ways You Can Save 1000s of Dollars).
    Seattle: Brier Books, 1992.

Dickson, Paul.
    The Official Rules.
    New York: Delacorte Press, 1978.
—. *The Official Explanations.*
    New York: Delacorte Press, 1980.

Dominguez, Joe, and Vicki Robin.
Your Money or Your Life: Transforming Your Relationship with Money and Achieving Financial Independence
New York: Penguin Books, 1992.

Durning, Alan.
How Much Is Enough? The Consumer Society and the Future of the Earth.
New York: W. W. Norton & Company, 1992.

Elgin, Duane.
Voluntary Simplicity.
New York: Morrow, revised edition 1993.

Ellmen, Eugene.
The 1997 Canadian Ethical Money Guide.
Halifax: Lorimer, 1996.

Ferguson, Marilyn.
The Aquarian Conspiracy.
Los Angeles: J. P. Tarcher, Inc., 1980.

Galbraith, John Kenneth.
The Affluent Society.
Boston: Houghton Mifflin, 1958.

Godfrey, Neale S. with Ted Richards.
From Cradle to College: A Parent's Guide to Financing Your Child's Life.
New York: HarperCollins, 1996.

Gregg, Richard.
The Value of Voluntary Simplicity. [a 31-page essay]
Pendle Hill, 1936.

Henderson, Bill, editor.
Minutes of the Lead Pencil Club.
Wainscott, New York: Pushcart Press, 1996.

Kinder, Peter, Steven Lindenberg and Amy Domini.
Investing for Good – making money while being socially responsible.
New York: HarperBusiness, 1993.

Korten, David C.
When Corporations Rule the World.
West Hartford, CN: Kumarian Press, and
San Francisco, CA: Berret-Koehler Publishers, 1995, 1996.

Leopold, Aldo.
  A Sand County Almanac with essays on conservation from Round River.
  Copyright 1966 by Oxford University Press Inc.
  This edition (New York: Ballantine Books, 1970) published by agreement with
  Oxford University Press.

Long, Charles.
  How to Survive Without a Salary: Learning How to Live the Conserver Lifestyle.
  Toronto, Los Angeles: Warwick Publishing, 1996.

Longacre, Doris Janzen.
  Living More with Less.
  Scottsdale, Pennsylvania/Waterloo, Ontario: Herald Press, 1995.

McQuaig, Linda.
  Shooting the Hippo: Death by Deficit and Other Canadian Myths.
  Toronto: Viking, Penguin Books Canada, 1995.

Needleman, Jacob.
  Money and the Meaning of Life.
  New York: Doubleday, 1991.

Norman, Donald A.
  Turn Signals Are the Facial Expressions of Automobiles.
  Reading, MA: Addison-Wesley Publishing Company, Inc., 1992.

Pogue, Carolyn, editor.
  *Treasury of Celebrations: Create Celebrations that Reflect Your Values and Don't
  Cost the Earth.*
  Kelowna, BC: Northstone Publishing Inc., 1996.

Popcorn, Faith and Lys Marigold.
  Clicking.
  New York: HarperBusiness, 1995.

Rheingold, Howard, editor.
  *The Millennium Whole Earth Catalog: Access to Tools & Ideas for the Twenty-First
  Century*
  New York: HarperSanFrancisco. Copyright 1994 by Point Foundation.

Rushkoff, Douglas.
  Media Virus!
  New York: Ballantine Books, 1994.

Saltzman, Amy.
    Downshifting: Reinventing Success on a Slower Track.
    New York: HarperCollins, 1991.

St. James, Elaine.
    Simplify Your Life: 100 Ways to Slow Down and Enjoy the Things
    That Really Matter.
    New York: Hyperion, 1994.
—. *Inner Simplicity: 100 Ways to Regain Peace and Nourish Your Soul.*
    New York: Hyperion, 1995.
—. *Living the Simple Life.*
    New York: Hyperion, 1996.

Scher, Les and Carol Scher.
    Finding and Buying Your Place in the Country.
    Chicago, IL: Dearborn Financial Publishing, 1992.

Schumacher, E. F.
    Small Is Beautiful: Economics as if People Mattered.
    New York: Harper & Row, 1973.

Selye, Hans.
    The Stress of Life.
    New York, Toronto: McGraw Hill Book Company, 1956.

Shi, David E.
    The Simple Life.
    New York: Oxford University Press, 1986.

Waring, Marilyn.
    Three Masquerades: Essays on Equality, Work and Human Rights.
    Toronto: University of Toronto Press, 1997.
—. *If Women Counted: A New Feminist Economics.*
    New York: HarperCollins, 1990

Wilson, Edward O.
    The Diversity of Life.
    Cambridge, MA: The Belknap Press of Harvard University Press, 1992.

Wylie, Betty Jane.
   Family.
   Kelowna, BC: Northstone Publishing Inc., 1997.
—. *Beginnings: A Book for Widows.* (third ed.)
   Toronto: McClelland & Stewart, 1997.
—, with Christopher Cottier.
   The Best Is Yet to Come: Enjoying a Financially Secure Retirement.
   Toronto: Key Porter Books, 1996.
—, with Lynne Macfarlane.
   Everywoman's Money Book. (fifth ed.)
   Toronto: Key Porter Books, 1995.

Index